PULSE-WIDTH MODULATED BRIDGELESS DC-DC CONVERTERS

A DETAILED ANALYSIS ON CUK CONVERTERS

ANJAN KUMAR SAHOO

Made with ♥ on the Notion Press Platform
www.notionpress.com

Contents

Preface

This is the most important and necessary subject in the area of science and technology. It is taught as an advanced subject in almost all Engineering Institutions and Universities irrespective of any branch. This book is more useful for research scholars, M.Tech and PhD students. Students having basic knowledge on power electronics and control can get more benefits from this book.

The authors shall feel grateful if the book meets the need of students for whom it is meant. Suggestions for the improvement of the book shall be welcomed. The authors would like to thank all the Engineers, Authors and Publishers whose works and text have been the source of enlightenment, inspiration and guidance.

Anjan Kumar Sahoo

Girija Sankar Panigrahi

About The Author

Enter Caption

Prof. Anjan Kumar Sahoo is working as an Assistant Professor in Department of Electrical Engineering at College of Engineering Bhubaneswar, Odisha India. He is having more than 13 years of experience in teaching, research & Industry. He has a very good competency in teaching of many electrical and electronics papers of both UG and PG courses.

He has completed his B.Tech from Biju Patnaik University of Technology in the year 2007 and M.Tech in Control & Instrumentation from Motilal Nehru National Institute of Technology, Allahabad, India in 2013.Currently he is pursuing Ph.D. at Centurion University of Technology & Management. His research area is Transmission line fault analysis using Machine Learning.

He has till date published 15 Scopus and WoS indexed journals with good impact factor. He has also published 7 technical books and 1 book chapter. He has 2 more papers under review in SCOPUS Indexed journals. He has received Young Achiever's Award 2019 from INSc. He is the life member of many professional bodies like ISTE, AMIE, IFERP etc.

About The Author

Enter Caption

Prof.Girija Sankar Panigrahi received B.Tech degree in Electrical Engineering from I.G.I.T,Sarang,(Utkal University), Odisha, India in 1992, M.Tech degree in Power Electronics and Drives from SOA University, Bhubaneswar, Odisha, India in 2011 and currently he is pursuing Ph.D at I.T.E.R, Siksha 'O' Anusandhan University, Bhubaneswar, Odisha, India.

He is currently working as an Assistant Professor in the Department of Electrical Engineering at Modern Institute of Technology and Management, Bhubaneswar, Odisha, India. He is having teaching experience of around 18 years in UG and PG levels and 07 years of Industry experience. He has published 3 papers in International journals. His research area includes Application of Robust Control methods for performance enhancement of Distributed Power Generation systems, Renewable Energy Systems and Solar Micro grids.

CHAPTER ONE

Introduction

Switch mode power supplies are widely used in the power electronics & telecommunication applications. Nevertheless the converters with hard switching technique suffer from switching losses, very low efficiency and substantial amount of EMI. There are two ways to improve the efficiency [1] of the converter either by reducing the energy loss of each component or by introducing the soft switching technique [9]. The cuk converter based on soft switching technique is presented in [10-13].In [13] an attractive comparison between four different types of zero voltage transition cuk converters is made. In all these papers [10-13] soft switching is done in different ways but the presence of input diode bridge rectifier makes the conduction losses more. Fig. below shows conventional input diode bridge rectifier cuk converter. The numbers of elements used in each switching cycle are more. This results more conduction losses and less efficiency, although it is of low cost and simple in construction. As we are more interested in the improvement of efficiency, we have to design a bridgeless converter with soft switching technique.

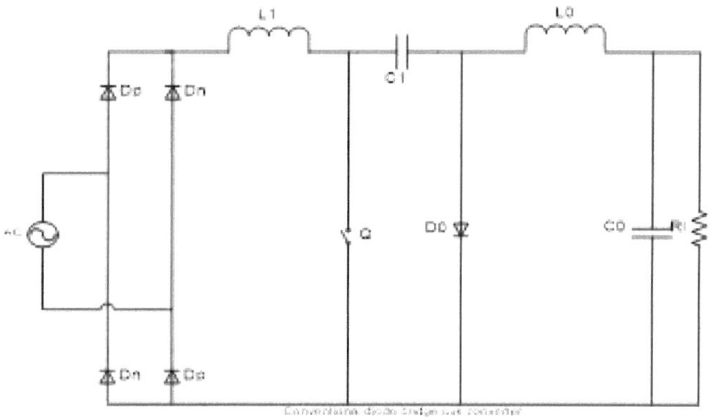

Conventional Diode bridge CUK converter

These days the bridgeless converter has obtained its popularity in designing switch mode power supplies.Fig. below shows the cuk converter [15].Due to the bridgeless structure and soft switching technique, the efficiency of the converter is very high but this boost type converter suffers from many drawbacks like

(1) the dc output voltage is always higher than the peak input voltage,

(2) implementation of input-output isolation is difficult,

(3) the startup inrush current is high and there is lack of current limiting during overload condition [3].

To overcome the problems associated with boost converter, a bridgeless step down cuk converter with soft switching technique is proposed in this book.

Soft switching condition is achieved for all semiconductor elements without any significant additional voltage or current stresses. To reduce the voltage and current stresses on the switching devices and improve the converter efficiency, soft switching technique for the proposed converter is applied by providing the auxiliary circuit. The auxiliary circuit consists of one switch, one resonant inductor and two resonant capacitors. The zero voltage switching (ZVS) turn on or zero current switching (ZCS) turn off is achieved by using resonant converter [4-7] based on resonant inductor and resonant capacitor. The control signal obtained by taking a portion of the output voltage is provided to the gate drive. This is done to regulate the output voltage and hence improve the efficiency.

The analysis on the efficiency of different switching devices with respect to output power is made in [3]. It says that efficiency improvement is more articulated when an IGBT is used as the switching device. The proposed converter follows the same for efficiency improvement. All switches are PWM controlled and operate in soft switching mode. The converter has high efficiency and produces little electromagnetic interference.

CHAPTER TWO

Literature Review

In this chapter we will go for a complete discussion on each and every part of our proposed converter individually. The reason of choosing the cuk converter, bridgeless structure, pulse width modulation technique, soft switching technique etc.

The CUK converter

The cuk converter is one member of flyback family named after Slobodan cuk who first presented. It is an inverting converter, so the output voltage is negative w.r.t. Input voltage. The main energy storing element is capacitor unlike the inductor in other converters. Cuk converter is actually the cascade combination of a boost and a buck converter.

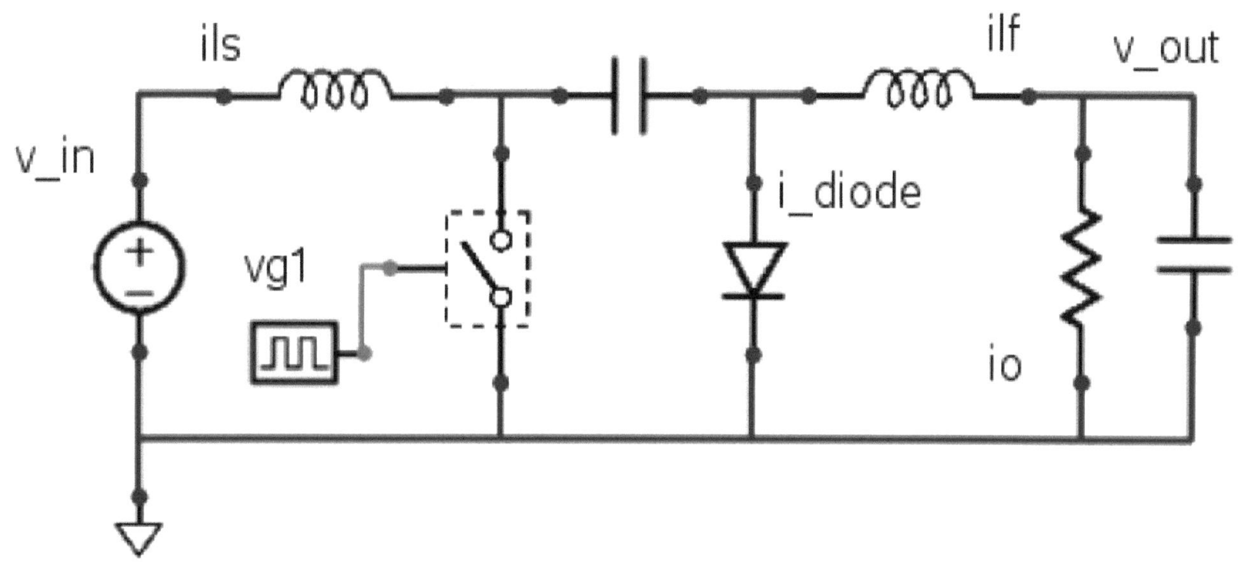

CUK converter

It has following advantages:

- Continuous input & output current.
- Output voltage can be either greater or less than input voltage.
- Low inductor ripple current.
- The input and output inductors result in a filtered current on both sides of the converter, while buck, boost, and buck-boost converters have a pulsating current that occurs on at least one side of the circuit.
- This pulsation will increase the ripple in the circuit and due to this ripple, the efficiency of battery gets lowered. To ensure good efficiency ripple should be reduced.

- By controlling the duty cycle of the switch, the output voltage Vo can be controlled and can be higher or lower than the input voltage vg.
- By using a controller to vary the duty cycle during operation, the circuit can also be made to reject disturbances, as second part of circuit consists of parallel resonance circuit and it work as a tank circuit for specific resonant frequency.

The main applications of this converter are in regulated dc power supplies, where a negative polarity output may be desired with respect to the common terminals of the input voltage and the average output is either higher or lower than the dc input voltage.

CHARACTERISTICS	BOOST	BUCK-BOOST	SEPIC	CUK
INDUCTOR POSITION	GOOD	BAD	GOOD	GOOD
I/P O/P ISOLATION	DIFFICULT	EASY	EASY	EASY
O/P VOLTAGE V_0	$>V_{in}$	ANY	ANY	ANY
START UP CAPABILITY	NO, Auxiliary	INHERENT	INHERENT	INHERENT
OVER CURRENT CONTROL	NO	YES	YES	YES
SWITCH VOLTAGE	V_0	$V_0+V_{in\,max}$	$V_0+V_{in\,max}$	$V_0+V_{in\,max}$

Characteristic comparison of different converters

Bridged and bridgeless rectifier

This type of single phase rectifier uses four individual rectifying diodes connected in a closed loop "bridge" configuration to produce the desired output. The main advantage of this bridge circuit is that it does not require a special center tapped transformer, thereby reducing its size and cost. The single secondary winding is connected to one side of the diode bridge network and the load to the other side as shown below. The four diodes labeled D_1 to D_4 are arranged in "series pairs" with only two diodes conducting current during each half cycle. During the positive half cycle of the supply, diodes D1 and D2 conduct in series while diodes D3 and D4 are reverse biased and the current flows through the load as shown below.

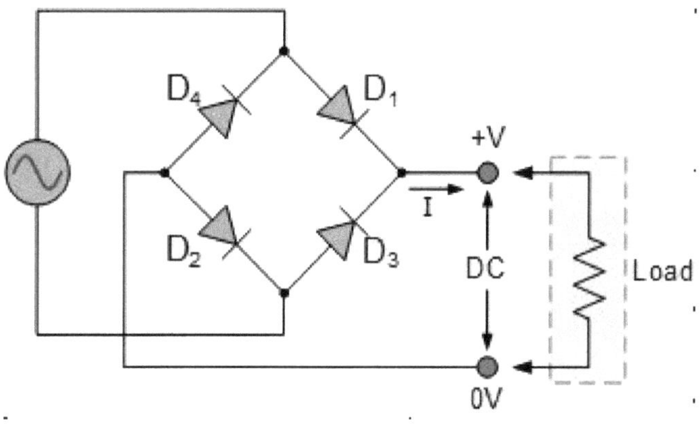

Diode Bridge Rectifier

The diode bridge rectifier is having following disadvantages:

The main problem with a diode bridge is the fact that we always have two diodes in series with our circuit, and this creates a voltage drop of about 1.4 V between the power source and the load. The power loss is simply this voltage drop multiplied by the load current. It also means that we cannot connect the negative side of the load, which we might ordinarily consider to be "ground", to any external ground, which might be connected to either side of the power source.

- High input current harmonics
- High conduction loss
- High ripple factor,
- Low rectification efficiency,
- Low transformer utilization factor, and,
- DC saturation of transformer secondary winding.

Due to the above demerits of the bridged circuit, we go for the bridgeless topology. It overcomes those demerits. As a result of which the input current harmonics is reduced. The conduction losses are reduced and ultimately the efficiency and power factor is improved. The proposed bridgeless topology has fewer semiconductors in the current conduction path over the whole switching cycle. However, it has one additional switch compared with the conventional Cuk. Nonetheless, the switching losses are the same because only one switch is active over a switching cycle. The current stress in the output diode of the proposed rectifier is less because it conducts only over half line cycle. Also, the proposed rectifier has a floating switch which requires additional gating circuitry. A very clear objective to increase the efficiency is to devise a converter, which can eliminate a front-end full-bridge rectifier. Past attempts failed to eliminate diode-bridge rectifiers, leading to the belief that the solution to such a goal may in addition, the output voltage of the proposed topology are floating with respect to the input voltage.

Concept of hard switching & soft switching

Hard Switching Converters:

Hard Switching converters comprise of those converters which obeys the conventional switching phenomenon. While the switch is turned ON, the voltage across the switch tends to decrease and the current across the switch tends to increase. This results in some switching losses. Alike to turning ON, when the switch is turned OFF, the current through the switch tends to decrease and the voltage across its terminals tends to increase. This too results in switching losses. There are several topologies [17] of these conventional hard switching converters of which we discuss mainly 6 types of converters in the form of comparison:

DC-DC Converter	Number of switches	Range of average output voltage	average output voltage	Relationship between the duty cycle and output voltage
Buck	One	0-V_i	D V_{in}	Linear
Boost	One	V_i-8	D/(1-D) V_{in}	Non- Linear
Buck-Boost	Two	0-V_i& V_i-8	- D/(1-D) V_{in}	Non- Linear
Cuk	One	0-V_i& V_i-8	- D/(1-D) V_{in}	Non- Linear
Sepic	One	0-V_i& V_i-8	- D^2/(1-D) V_{in}	Non- Linear

HARD SWITCHING DC-DC CONVERTER TOPOLOGIES

Concept of Soft switching

Conventional PWM converters operate on hard switching phenomenon where voltage and current pulses, during their transition from high to low values or low to high values interact with each other and cause power losses called switching losses and generate a substantial amount of electromagnetic interference [18]. Switching losses arise because of output capacitor of transistor, capacitance of diode, diode reverse recovery. It is observed that switching losses are proportional to switching frequency. So, higher switching losses lead to the limitation of switching frequency. Because of a wide spectral range of harmonics present in PWM waveform, a high Electro Magnetic Interference (EMI) occurs. EMI also results from high current spikes caused by diode recovery.

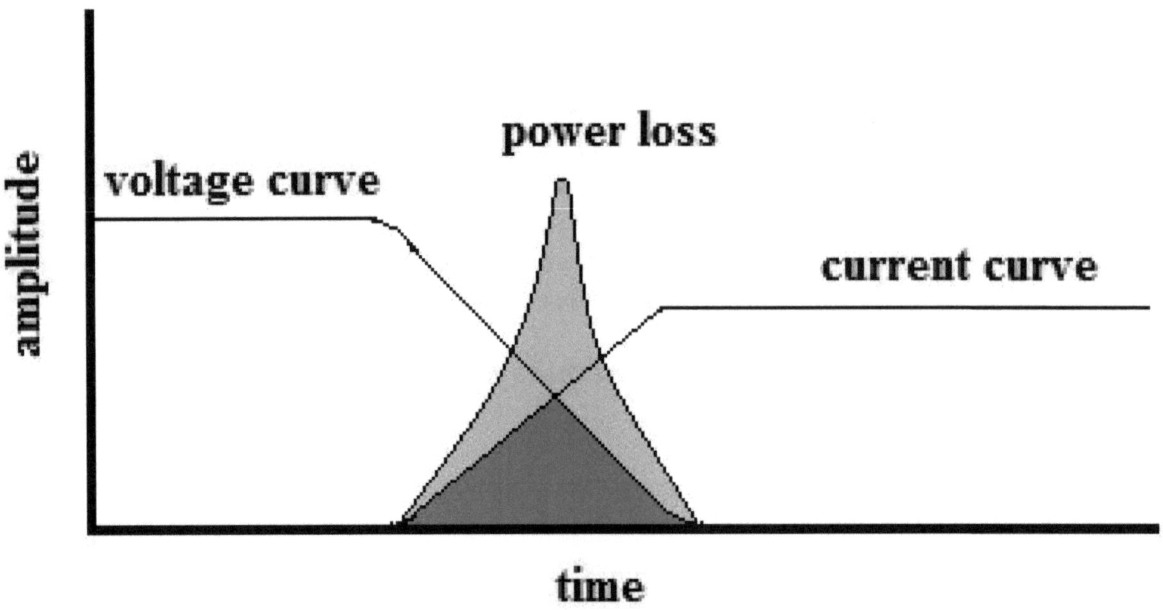

HARD SWITCHING PHENOMENON

Switching losses and EMI can be reduced by using soft switching techniques at the expense of stress on the device. If the semiconductor device is made to turn off or turn on when current or voltage is zero, then the product of voltage and current during transition is zero which leads to zero power loss. Thus switching losses are eliminated and the device can be made to operate at high switching frequencies. Size and weight of the device also reduce because of non-requirement of heat sink.

The soft switching techniques are widely categorized into two types namely:

- Zero Voltage Switching (ZVS)
- Zero Current Switching (ZCS)

Zero Voltage Switching (ZVS)

The technique in which the MOSFET or any other semiconductor turns on at zero voltage is called ZVS.

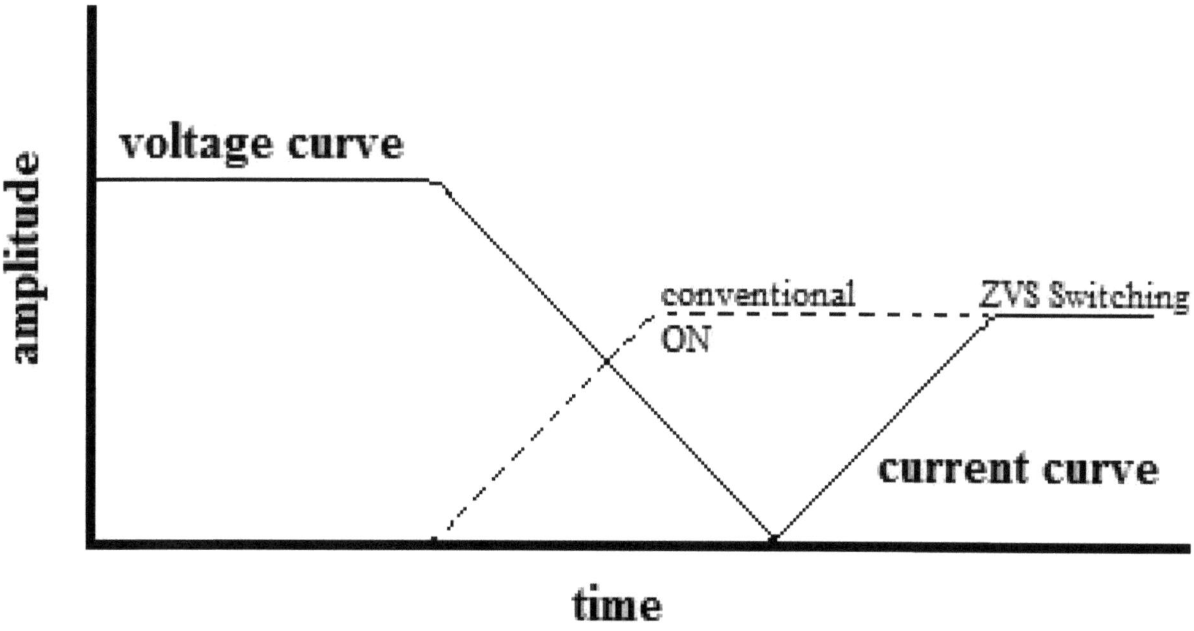

ZERO VOLTAGE SWITCHING (ZVS)

The ZVS is used during the turn on of the device. Initially the main MOSFET S is off and the auxiliary MOSFET S1 is on. So the current through main switch is zero, whereas voltage is not zero. During the turn on voltage is made zero across the switch and current is given some time delay such that current begins to rise after the voltage becomes zero. This is called ZVS.

Zero Current Switching (ZCS)

The technique in which MOSFET or any other semiconductor device turns off at zero current is called ZCS. ZCS is used during turn off of the device. Initially the device is conducting. So the current passing through the device is not zero and the voltage across the device is zero. In the ZCS condition, current is made zero and the voltage is made to rise only after the current becomes zero. Thus, there is no power loss during turn off of the device.

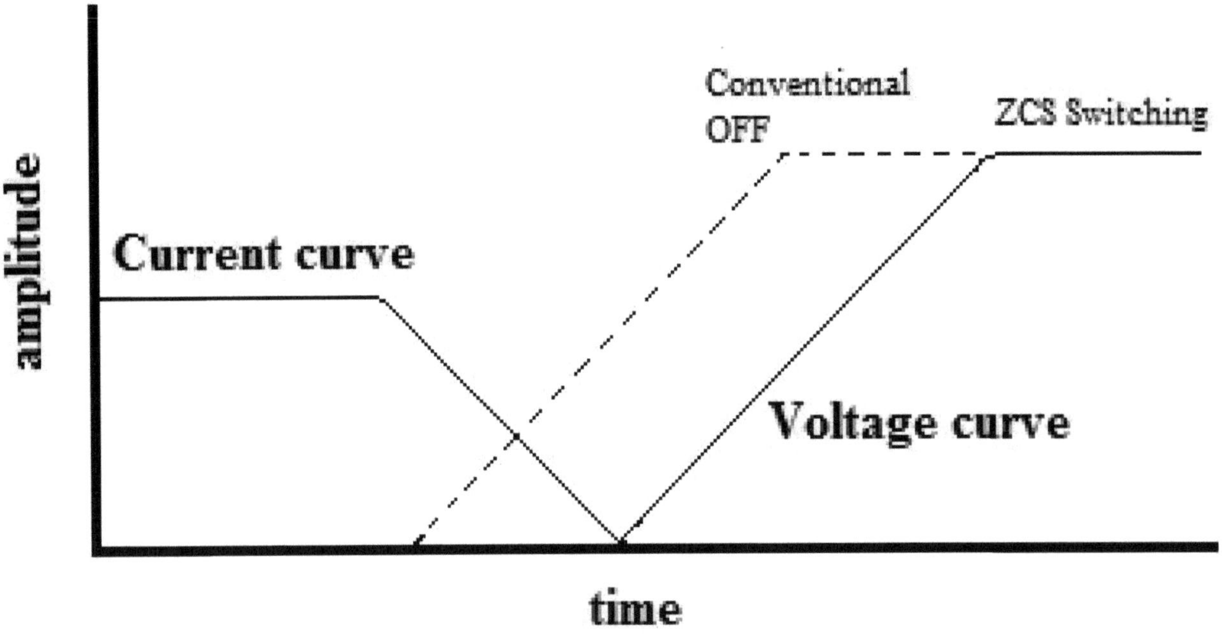

Zero Current Switching (ZCS)

Concept and requirement of Pulse Width Modulation (PWM)

Pulse width modulation (PWM) is a powerful technique for controlling analog circuits with a microprocessor digital outputs. PWM is employed in a wide variety of applications, ranging from measurement and communications to power control and conversion.

Analogue circuits

An analogue signal has a continuously varying value, with infinite resolution in both time and magnitude. A nine-volt battery is an example of an analog device, in that its output voltage is not precisely 9V, changes over time, and can take any real-numbered value. Analogue signals are distinguishable from digital signals because the latter always takes values only from a finite set of predetermined possibilities, such as the set {0V, 5V}.

Analogue voltages and currents can be used to control things directly, like the volume of a car radio. With a simple analogue radio, a knob is connected to a variable resistor. As you turn the knob, the resistance goes up or down. As that happens, the current flowing through the resistor increases or decreases. This changes the amount of current driving the speakers, thus increasing or decreasing the volume. An analogue circuit is one, like the radio, whose output is linearly proportional to its input.

Digital control

By controlling analogue circuits digitally, system costs and power consumption can be drastically reduced.

In a nutshell, PWM is a way of digitally encoding analogue signal levels. Through the use of high-resolution counters, the duty cycle of a square wave is modulated to encode a specific analogue signal level. The PWM signal is still digital because, at any given instant of time, the full DC supply is either fully on or fully off. The voltage or current source is supplied to the analog load by means of a repeating series of on and off pulses. The on-time is the time during which the DC supply is applied to the load, and the off-time is the period during which that supply is switched off.

The figure shows three different PWM signals. Also figure shows a PWM output at a 10% duty cycle. That is, the signal is on for 10% of the period and off the other 90%. Figures show PWM outputs at 50% and 90% duty cycles, respectively. These three PWM outputs encode three different analogue signal values, at 10%, 50%, and 90% of the full strength. If, for example, the supply is 9V and the duty cycle is 10%, a 0.9V analogue signal result.

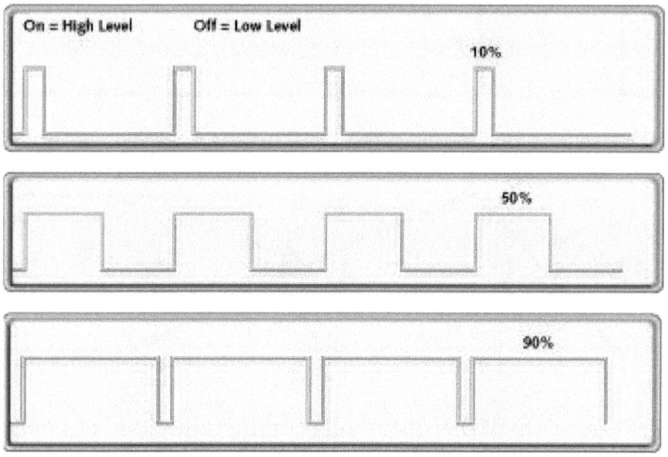

PWM signals of varying duty cycles

Merits and Demerits of DCM and CCM

Discontinuous conduction mode (DCM)

- Used for low power levels <=300w.It has high peak currents that limits its use at higher input power levels.
- The o/p voltage decreases with increase in load current.
- Conduction and switching losses are more.
- Output impedance is more.
- Efficiency is less.
- It has an explicit RL dependence.

Only voltage follower method is possible.

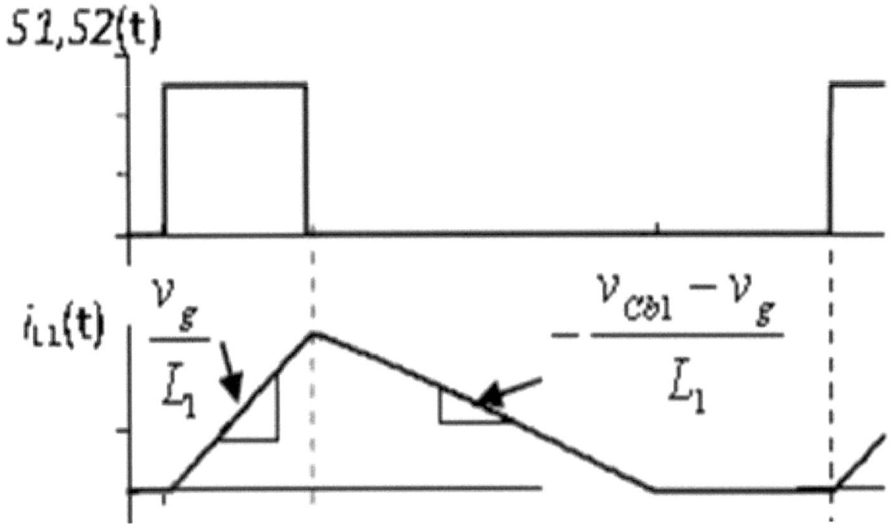

Key waveform of discontinuous conduction mode of operation

Continuous conduction mode (CCM)

- Used for high power levels >300w.This lowers the peak current seen by the power switch and output rectifier.
- The load voltage depends only on the firing angle and not on load parameters.
- Conduction and switching losses are less.
- Output impedance is less.
- Efficiency is more.
- No effect on load resistance.

Except voltage follower, other methods are possible.

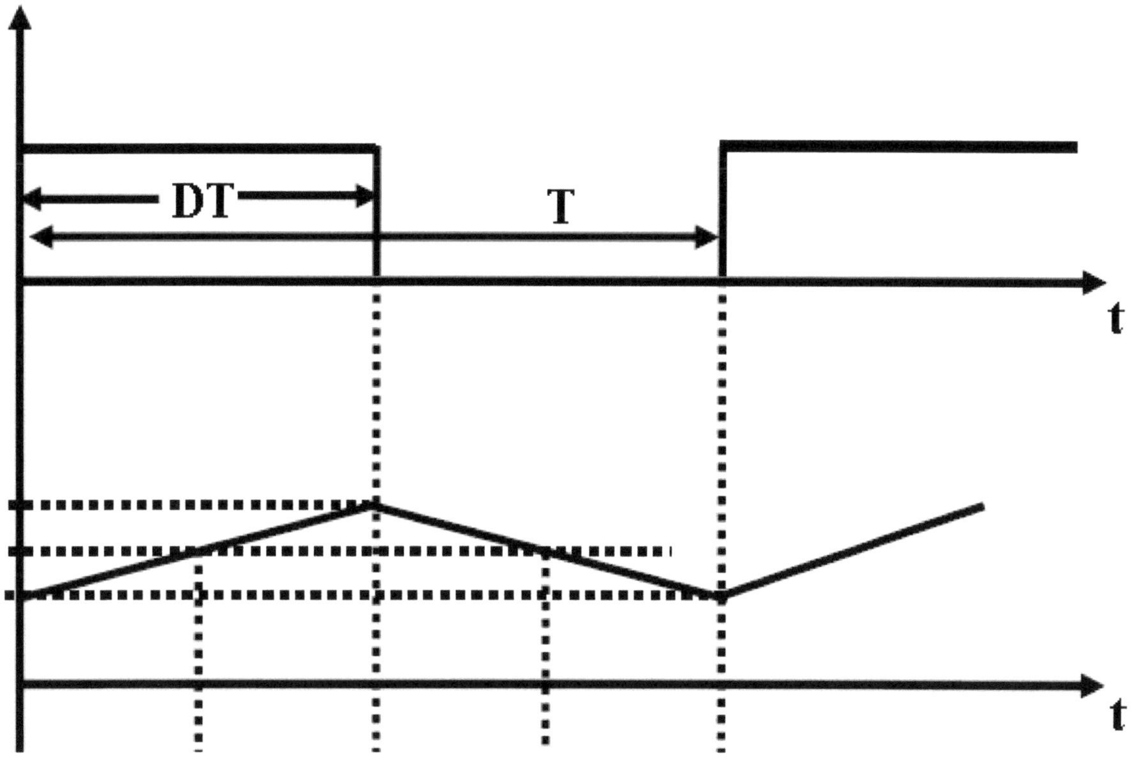

Key waveform of continuous conduction mode of operation

Due to the above demerits of DCM, our converter operates in CCM.

Control Strategies

Control schemes are needed to get a controlled and desired response. The control schemes are applied depending upon the converter mode of operation as discussed in the previous paragraph. There are different types of control schemes such as:

- Voltage mode control,
- Multiplier control,
- Peak current control,
- Average current mode control,
- One cycle control.

Each has its own merits and demerits. The most detailed of each controller is discussed below.

Voltage mode control

Here as shown in the figure below the converter output voltage that is to be regulated is sensed and feedback through a resistive voltage divider. It is then compared with a precision external reference voltage, V_{ref} in a voltage error amplifier. The error amplifier produces a control voltage that is compared to a constant-amplitude sawtooth waveform. The comparator or the PWM Modulator produces a PWM signal that is fed to drivers of controllable switches in the DC-DC converter. The duty ratio of the PWM signal depends on the value of the control voltage. The frequency of the PWM signal is the same as the frequency of the sawtooth waveform.

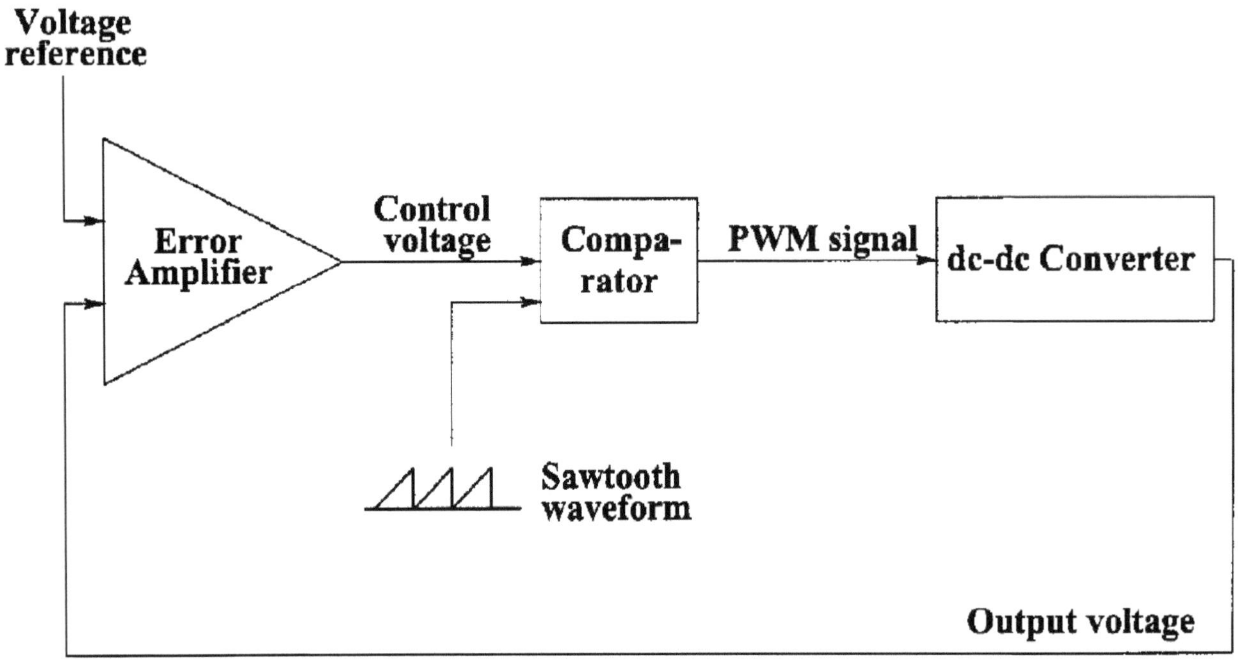

Schematic diagram of voltage follower control

Advantages:

- The simple hardware implementation and flexibility is the greatest advantage of voltage mode control scheme.
- The error amplifier keeps a fast track of changes in the converter output voltage. Thus, it provides good load regulation, that is, regulation against variations in the load.
- It is applied to the converters operated in DCM.

Disadvantages:

- This scheme has a poor line regulation i.e. Regulation against variations in the input voltage.
- It is delayed since any change in the input voltage must manifest itself in the converter output before it can be corrected.

It can't be applied to the converters operated in CCM.

Multiplier control approach

Signals in current form have a natural advantage over voltage signals. The voltage being an accumulation of electron flux is slow in time as far as control mechanism is concerned. This led to the development of a new area in switch mode power supply design, i.e. the Multiplier control method. It has given new avenues of analysis and at the same time introduced complexities in terms of multiple loops.

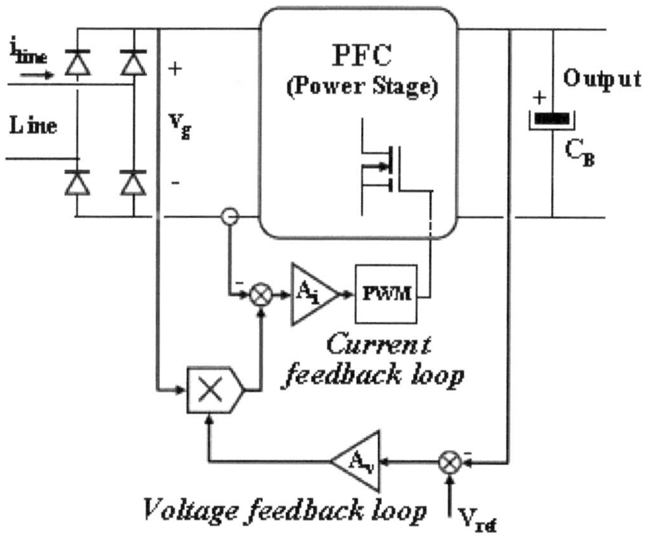

Schematic diagram of multiplier control approach

Merits of Multiplier control over voltage follower approach:

- The performance merits of current mode control over voltage mode control can be appreciated more by looking at the transient response when the converter is subjected to a step load disturbance or a step line change.
- Multiplier control approach can be applied to converters operated in CCM or DCM unlike voltage follower method.
- *One demerit of Multiplier method is its complicated circuit.*

Peak current control:

The objective of the inner loop is to control the state-space averaged inductor current, but in practice the instantaneous peak inductor current is the basis for control. The switch current during the ON time is equal to the inductor current. If the inductor ripple current is small, peak current control is nearly equivalent to the average inductor current control.

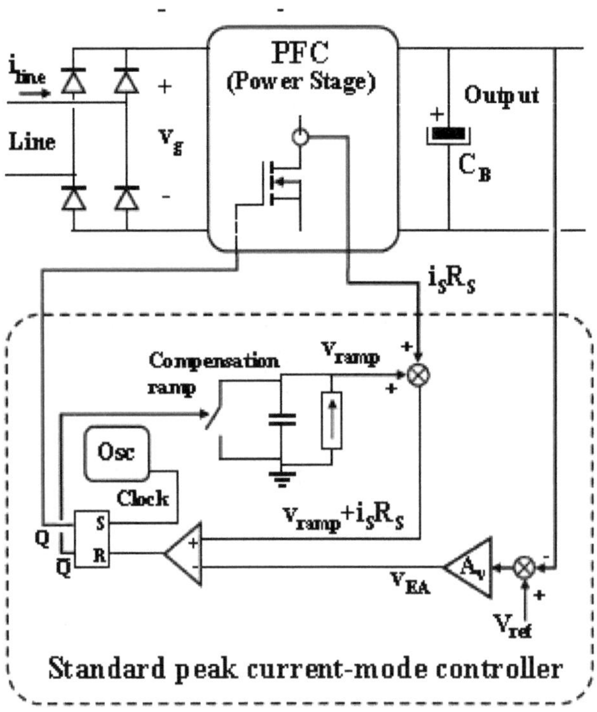

Schematic diagram of Peak current control approach

Merits:

- The input current feedback loop is extremely fast.
- It can be used for high frequency line

Peak current mode control problems:

Poor noise immunity: The peak method of inductor current control functions by comparing the upslope of inductor current (or switch current) to a current program level set by the outer loop-see Fig. 12. The comparator turns the power switch off when the instantaneous current reaches the desired level. The current ramp is usually quite small compared to the programming level, especially when Vin is low.

As a result, this method is extremely susceptible to noise. A noise spike is generated each time the switch turns on. A fraction of a volt coupled into the control circuit can cause it to turn off immediately, resulting in a sub-harmonic operating mode with much greater ripple. Circuit layout and bypassing are critically important to successful operation.

Slope compensation required: The peak current mode control method is inherently unstable at duty ratios exceeding 0.5, resulting in sub-harmonic oscillation. A compensating ramp (with slope equal to the inductor current down slope) is usually applied to the comparator input to eliminate this instability. In a buck regulator the inductor current down slope equals V0/L. With V0 constant, as it usually is, the compensating ramp is fixed and easy to calculate-but it does complicate the design. With a boost regulator in a high power factor application, the down slope of inductor current equals $(V_{in}-V_0)/L$ and thus varies considerably as the input voltage follows the rectified sine waveform. A fixed ramp providing adequate compensation will overcompensate much of the time, with resulting performance degradation and increased distortion.

- It has a wide bandwidth which makes it unsuitable for a high performance PFC since there is a significant error between the programming signal and current which leads to distortion and a poor power factor.

- It has a low gain.

Average current mode control: Peak current mode control operates by directly comparing the actual inductor current waveform to the current program level (set by the outer loop) at the two inputs of the PWM comparator. This current loop has low gain and so cannot correct for the deficiencies.

Referring to Figure below the technique of average current mode control overcomes these problems by introducing a high gain integrating current error amplifier *(CA)* into the current loop. A voltage across ***Rp,*** (set by the outer loop) represents the desired current program level. The voltage across current sense resistor ***Rs,*** represents actual inductor current. The difference, or current error, is amplified and compared to a large amplitude saw tooth (oscillator ramp) at the PWM comparator inputs.

For Average current-mode control there are three things to consider:

1. Current-mode operation. An ideal current-mode converter is only dependent on the dc or average inductor current. The inner current loop turns the inductor into a voltage controlled current source, effectively removing the inductor from the outer voltage control loop at dc and low frequency.
2. Modulator gain. The modulator gain is dependent on the effective slope of the ramp presented to the modulating comparator input. Each operating mode will have a unique characteristic equation for the modulator gain.
3. Slope compensation. The requirement for slope compensation is dependent on the relationship of the average current to the value of current at the time when the sample is taken. For fixed-frequency operation, if the sampled current were equal to the average current, there would be no requirement for slope compensation.

As shown in the figure below, average current mode control (ACMC) is a two loop control method. This control method has many applications in the higher switching frequency, lower power segment up to 10kW, at higher switching frequency and above. It is frequently being used for the control of DC/DC converters and single phase Power factor correctors.

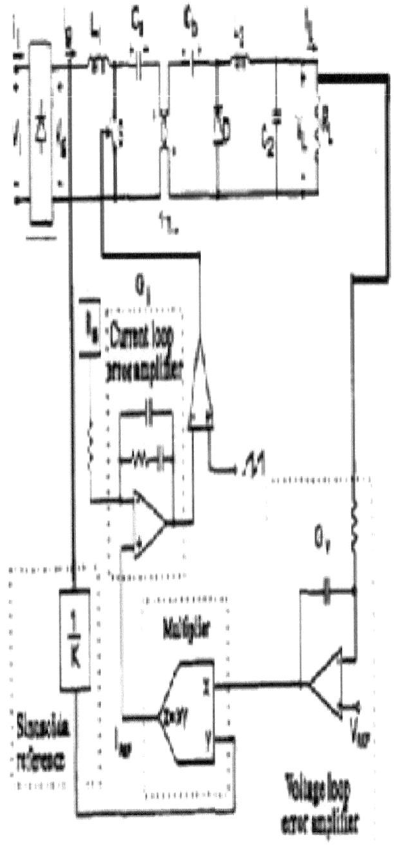

Schematic diagram of average current control approach

Merits:

- Better line regulation is achieved using ACMC.
- It operates with a constant switching frequency.
- Here no compensation ramp is required.
- Since the current is filtered the control is less sensitive to commutation noises unlike peak current mode control.

Demerits:

- The inductor current has to be sensed.
- Here a current error amplifier is required for which a compensation network has to be designed for different converter operating points.

Merits of average current mode control over peak current mode control:

i. An external compensation ramp is not required.
ii. Increased DC closed loop gain at low frequencies.
iii. Improved immunity to noise in the sensed current signal.
iv. The increased current loop DC gain at low frequencies is especially useful for single phase PFC applications using boost derived topologies. This is because here it is desirable that the average rather than the peak of the inductor current follows sinusoidal reference.

One cycle control:

The one cycle control technique is a technique which is very advantageous to all the converters except cuk converter. Because this technique becomes very complicated when we apply it to cuk converter. Still, it is having some unique merits as follows:

1. No multiplier requirement.
2. No inductor current sensing requirement.
3. By using one cycle control both voltage sensing and current sensing issues of the Bridgeless PFC circuit can be solved.

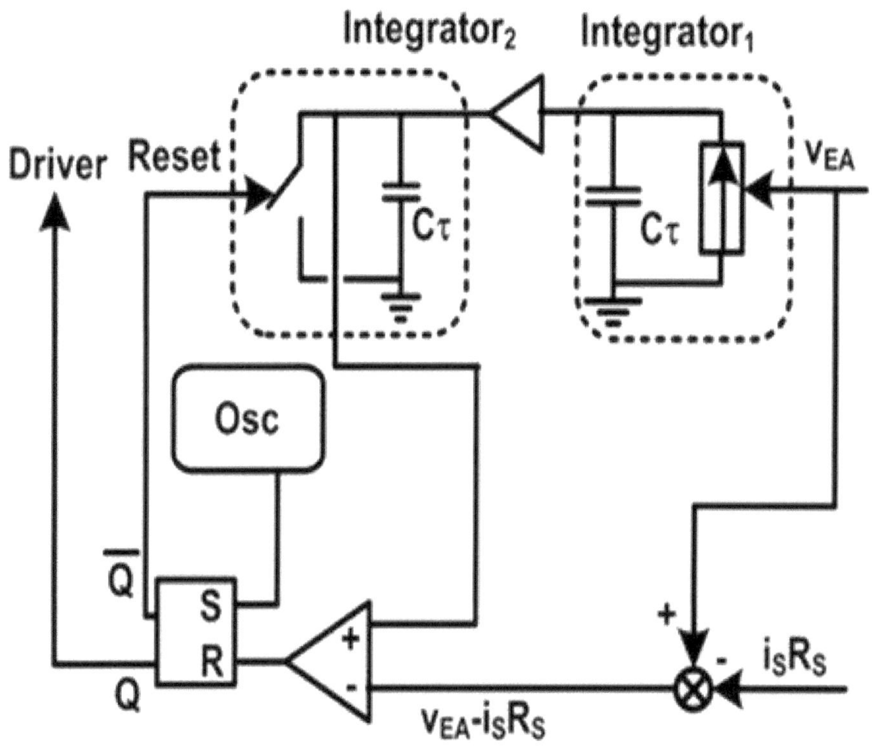

Schematic diagram of one cycle control approach

A boost type zero voltage switching (ZVS) isolated Cuk converter is presented in [5] to reduce the switching losses of main switch. As shown in figure below the ZVS operation of auxiliary switch is achieved by the resonance with the resonant inductor and the clamp capacitor. The converter is operated in continuous conduction mode.

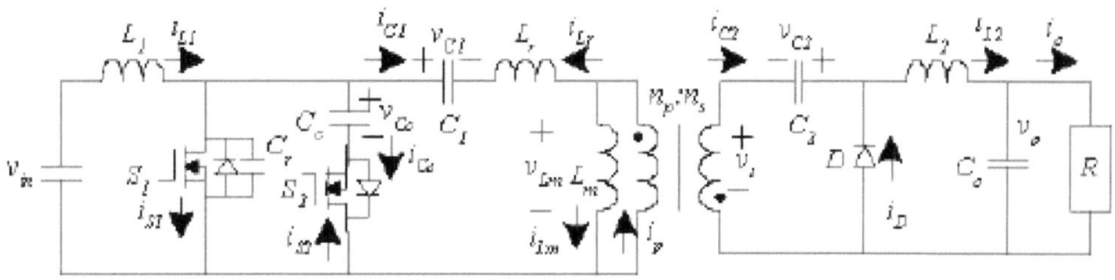

Schematic diagram of zero voltage switching (ZVS) isolated Cuk converter

The advantages of this type of converter are as follows:

The active clamp techniques based on auxiliary switch and clamp capacitor are proposed to reduce the voltage stress of the main switch and to increase efficiency of the converter. The active clamp converter uses the transformer leakage inductance and output capacitance of main switch to achieve resonance and to absorb the surge energy stored in the transformer leakage inductance. The measured efficiency of the proposed converter is 88% at the rated output power (12V/1.5A).

The demerit in this converter is that conduction and switching losses are little bit more due to the presence of the input diode bridge rectifier.

In [12] A zero-voltage switching parallel-connected Cuk converter is presented. The active snubber circuit is used in the converter to achieve soft switching and to limit voltage stress across power switches. Two half-wave rectifiers are connected in parallel at the output side to reduce the current stresses on the secondary winding of the transformer. The constant pulse-width modulation scheme is adopted to regulate the output voltage. A buck-boost stage active snubber circuit is used in the conventional isolated Cuk converter to allow the utilization of leakage inductance of the transformer, to achieve ZVS operation and to limit the voltage stresses on the power switches. The merits of this type of converter are as follows:

- Compared with the asymmetrical half-bridge converter, the proposed converter has less ripple currents on the input and output sides.
- The transformer primary voltage in the proposed converter is greater than the primary voltage in the asymmetrical half-bridge converter.

But the demerit is that the converter becomes bulky and complex. If we have any AC supply then we cannot use it directly. The author has made an analysis on cuk converter in [13]. The zero voltage transition is applied to cuk converter. Four classes of ZVT topologies and their advantages/disadvantages are explained for Cuk Converters. The merits obtained from this analysis are as follows:

- Power handling capability requirements of semiconductor devices of cuk converter are much higher than those of other topologies with the same output power.
- The Switch Utilization Factor(SUF) of the cuk topology is much lower than those of the buck topology and the boost topology. In [2] an efficient bridgeless cuk rectifier is presented. It operates in DCM to achieve almost a unity power factor and low THD of the input current. The advantages of this type converter are:
- The DCM operation gives additional advantages such as zero current turn on in power switches, zero current turn off in the output diode and the simple control circuitry.
- The proposed topologies don't suffer from high common mode EMI noise emission problem and have common mode EMI performance similar to the conventional PFC topologies.
- Thus the losses due to turn on switching and the reverse recovery of the output diodes are considerably reduced.

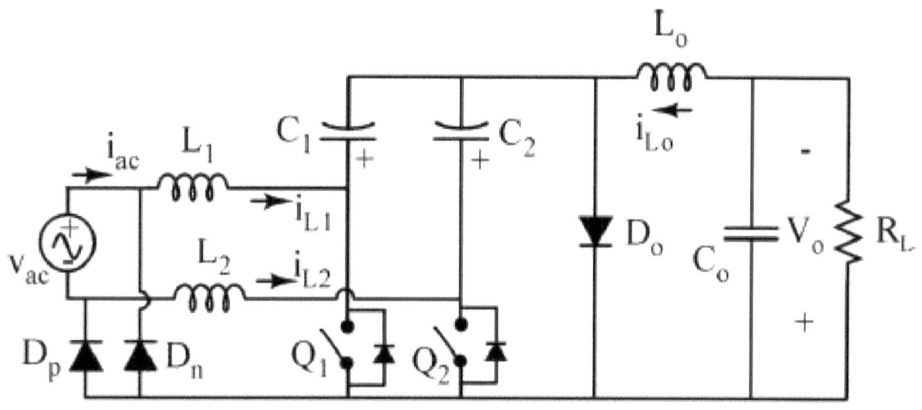

Bridgeless cuk pfc rectifier [2]

The limitation of this converter is that it topologies utilize one additional inductor, which is often described as a disadvantage in terms of size and cost.

A bridgeless Power Factor Correction (PFC) circuit based on the Cuk converter is proposed in [1]. The converter operates in discontinuous conduction mode. Voltage follower approach is used for the driver circuit.

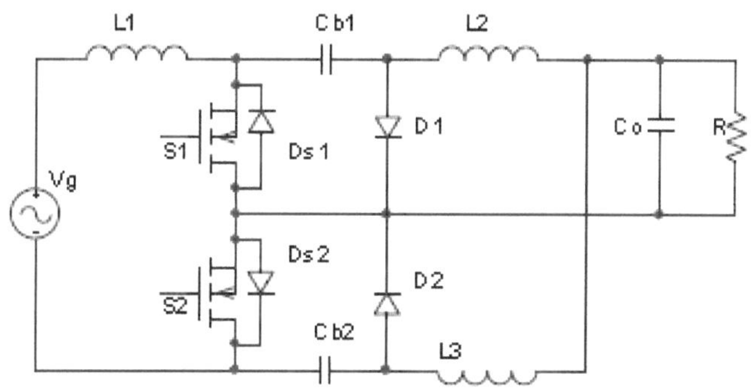

Schematic diagram of the bridgeless CUK PFC converter in DCM [1]

But the demerit here is that the switching loss of the converter is more due to the absence of soft switching technique. A bidirectional Cuk converter with active clamp is introduced in [10]. High frequency operation (100KHz) is done to reduce the reactive component size and cost. Soft switching condition is achieved for all semiconductor elements at both modes of operation without any significant additional voltage or current stresses. The advantages of this type converter are as follows:

- The bidirectional Cuk converter has the advantage of low ripple in input and output currents in addition to the ability of reversing the direction of current flow.
- The use of soft switching technique reduces the switching losses and electro-magnetic interference (EMI).

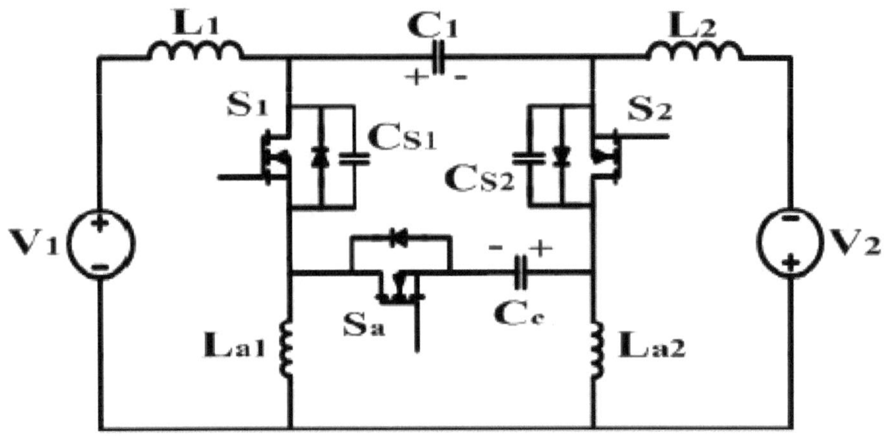

Schematic diagram of bidirectional Cuk converter

The bidirectional Cuk converter is a proper choice for applications like battery equalization and ultra capacitor-battery interface circuits which incorporate energy storage device (e.g. battery or super capacitor) and a bidirectional converter are applied to manage power flow and maintain energy storage devices health.

In [11] a new buck-boost type DC-DC converter is presented. This paper pays special attention to achieve the highest input power factor along with minimizing the input filter size of the proposed converter. For DC-DC purposes, the proposed converter can be attractive as a soft-switched alternative for SEPIC or Cuk converter. The merits obtained here are as follows:

- The filtering technique used in proposed circuit can be used for other Buck-boost type converters like SEPIC or CUK in discontinuous conduction mode.
- The proposed converter input current waveform is a smooth sinusoidal pulse, comparing to the sharp triangular current waveform of the conventional buck-boost type converters. Thus the produced switching harmonics are also smaller.

There is a trade-off between the power factor and ripple of the produced DC voltage. So this can be compensated by using an inductor & a capacitor of smaller size in following manner.

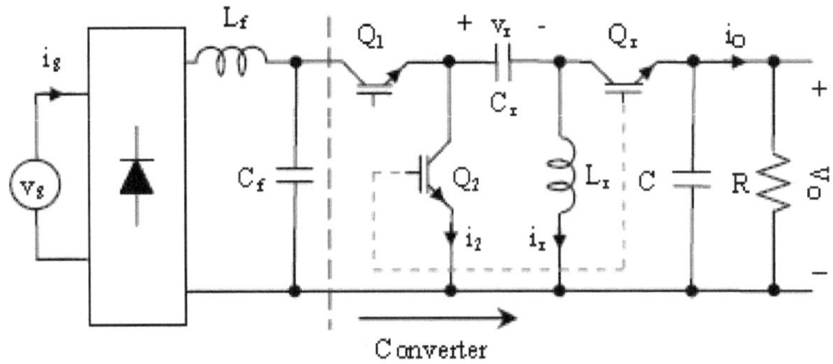

Schematic diagram of buck-boost type DC-DC converter [11]

An analysis and design on sepic and cuk power factor pre-regulator operated in DCM is made in [14]. As presented the desirable characteristics for a PFP are:

- The converter works as a voltage follower (no current loop is needed).
- Theoretical power factor is unity.
- The input current ripple is defined at the design stage.

This paper analyzes the operation of both converters as DCM-PFC.

A new bridgeless single phase ac-dc power factor correction (PFC) rectifiers based on sepic and cuk topologies are proposed in [3].The absence of an input diode bridge and the presence of only two semiconductor switches in the current flowing path during each switching cycle result in less conduction losses and improved thermal management compared to the conventional sepic and cuk pfc converters.

In [4] a new zero voltage transition bridgeless sepic pfc converter is introduced. Due to bridgeless structure, the conduction losses are very less and as a result efficiency is improved.

In [6] a number of soft-switching pulse-width-modulated (PWM) converter techniques have been proposed, aimed at combining the desirable features of both the conventional PWM and resonant converters while avoiding their respective limitations. In this paper, three classes of zero-voltage soft-switching (PWM) converters (namely the zero-voltage-switched (ZVS) quasi-square-wave converters, ZVS-PWM converters, and zero-voltage-transition PWM converters) and two classes of zero-current soft-switching PWM converters (namely, the zero-current-switched PWM converters and zero-current-transition PWM converters) are reviewed, and their merits and limitations are assessed. The author in this paper has discussed the advantages and disadvantages of adding an auxiliary switch across the resonant inductor in ZVS-QRC.

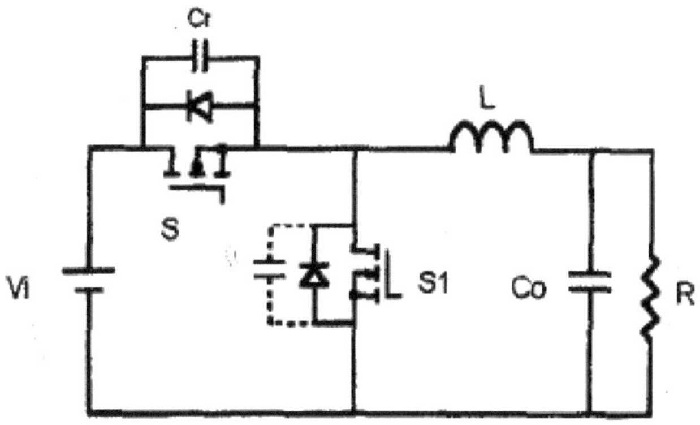

Schematic diagram of buck ZVS-QRC

The advantages are as follows:

- ZVS for the power switch.
- Low current stress on the power switch.

The disadvantages are as follows:

- High voltage stress on the power switch: One limitation of the single ended ZVS-PWM converters is that the power switch suffers from a high voltage stress that is proportional to the load range under which ZVS is maintained.
- The rectifier diode is not operated under favorable switching condition.

A new family of pulse width-modulated (PWM) converters, featuring soft commutation of the semiconductors at zero current (ZC) in the transistors and zero voltage (ZV) in the rectifiers is presented in [7]. Besides operating at constant frequency and with reduced commutation losses, these new converters have output characteristics similar to the hard-switching-PWM counterpart, which means that there is no circulating reactive energy that would cause large conduction losses. The new family of zero-current-switching (ZCS)-PWM converters are suitable for high-power applications using insulated gate bipolar transistors (IGBTs).

The advantages of the new ZCS-PWM boost converter employing IGBTs, rated at 1.6 kW and operating at 20 kHz, are presented. This new ZCS operation can reduce the average total power dissipation in the semiconductors practically by half, when compared with the hard-switching method. This new ZCS-PWM boost converter is suitable for high-power applications using IGBTs in power-factor correction.

Bridgeless boost PFC [8] is a concept that has been long on promise for many years, but has not reached mainstream acceptance. Issues with EMI, robustness and the complexity of early configurations have stymied efforts to realize the bridgeless boost PFC converter's potential. Furthermore, improvements in components used in standard PFC boost converters have resulted in efficiency gains that did not justify the extra cost and complexity of the bridgeless configuration. And while bridgeless PFC has been viewed as a potentially useful technique to improve low-line input efficiency.

A bridgeless boost rectifier with low conduction losses and reduced diode reverse-recovery problems [9] is proposed for power-factor correction. The proposed boost rectifier can reduce the conduction losses and alleviate the diode reverse-recovery problems by using a coupled inductor and two additional diodes. Zero-current turn-off of the output diodes is achieved, and the reverse-recovery currents of the additional diodes are slowed down to reduce the diode reverse-recovery losses. All inductive components are realized on a single magnetic core by utilizing the leakage inductance of the coupled inductor.

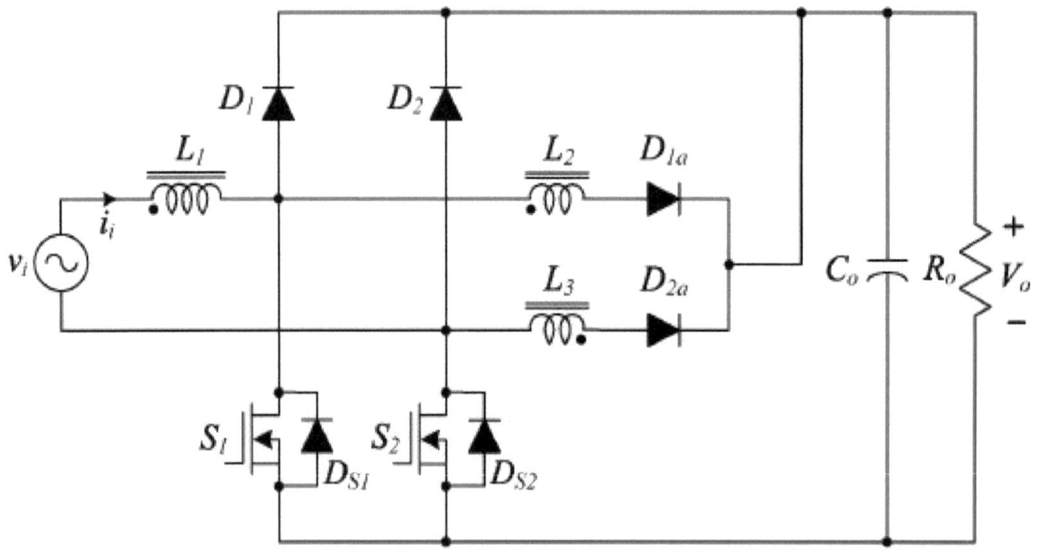

Schematic diagram of buck-boost type DC-DC converter

Furthermore, for the use of this topology in the practical design, the linear peak current mode control is employed for the proposed boost rectifier as shown in above figure.

SEPIC and Cuk converters present a great advantage over boost and fly-back topologies in discontinuous conduction mode (DCM): an input current with low harmonic content can be obtained by correctly choosing the inductors L_1 and L_2 of the converter with a fixed operation frequency, as is demonstrated in [16]. The authors also discuss the inter-medium capacitor C_1 as well as some advantages and disadvantages of the application. Simulation and experimental results support the approach. It is concluded that SEPIC and Cuk converters in DCM seem to be good choices for use as power factor pre-regulators.

The author has made an analysis of the bridgeless PFC circuit in [19].To reduce the converter bridge conduction loss, bridgeless circuit is employed, which provides simplicity and high performance as shown in the figure below. Without the input rectifier bridge, the bridgeless PFC generates less conduction loss compared with the conventional PFC.

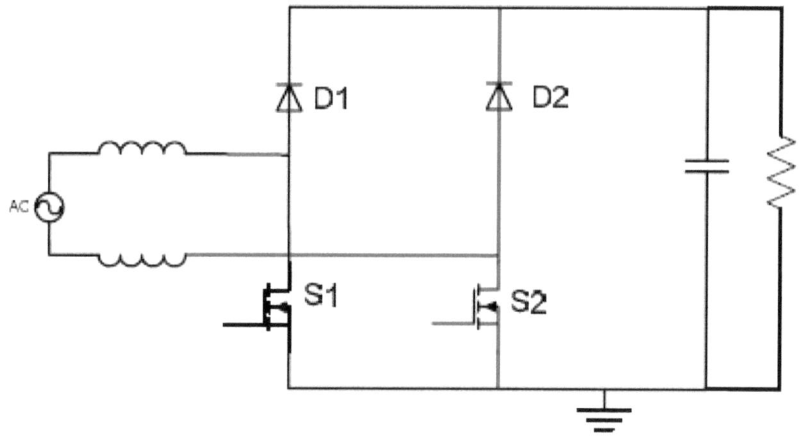

Schematic diagram of bridgeless PFC circuit

The advantages of using this converter are as follows:

- The diode conduction loss of bridgeless PFC is less than the conventional PFC.
- The loss percentage of the body diode and synchronous rectifier is almost same.
- The bridgeless PFC is more efficient than conventional PFC.
- But the EMI noise of bridgeless PFC is a little bit more than conventional PFC.
- Compared with the average current mode control, one cycle control shows many benefits such as no multiplier requirement, no input voltage sensing requirement and no inductor current sensing requirements.
- By using one cycle control both voltage sensing and current sensing issues of the bridgeless PFC circuit can be solved.

Basic buck, boost, buck-boost, fly back, forward, cuk, sepic and zeta converter topologies are investigated for PFC in [20].From the analysis, it is concluded that the CUK converter does not have good self PFC property in DCM. For that reason it is always advised to operate the cuk, sepic and zeta converters in DCM.

These days bridgeless converters with soft switching technique have gained its popularity in the power electronics and telecommunication applications. One of the most popular converters is a bridgeless boost converter with soft switching technique [15]. Fig. below shows the conventional bridgeless boost converter with soft switching technique.

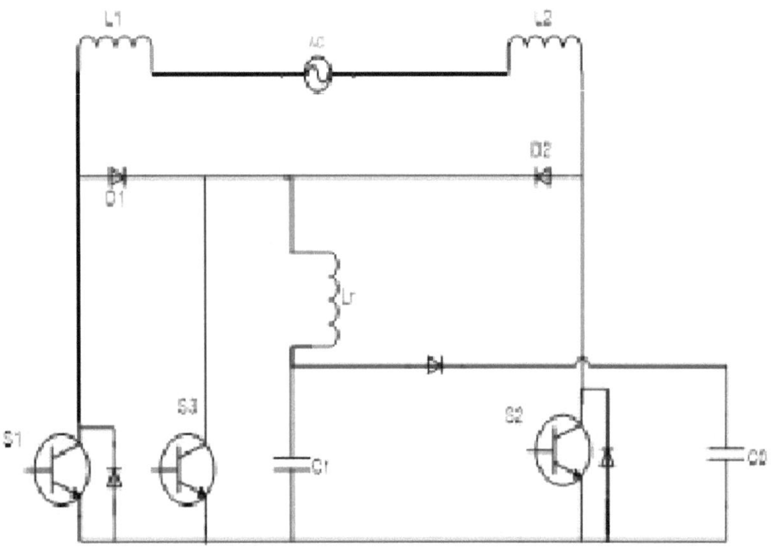

Conventional bridgeless boost converter with soft switching TECHNIQUE [15]

Due to the bridgeless structure and soft switching technique, the efficiency of the converter is very high but it suffers from many drawbacks like (1) the dc output voltage is always higher than the peak input voltage, (2) implementation of input-output isolation is difficult, (3) the startup inrush current is high and there is lack of current limiting during overload condition. The table below shows a comparison between the conventional boost converter and cuk converter.

CHARACTERISTICS	BOOST	CUK
INDUCTOR POSITION	GOOD	GOOD
I/P O/P ISOLATION	DIFFICULT	EASY
O/P VOLTAGE V0	>V in	ANY
OVER CURRENT CONTROL	NO	YES
SWITCH VOLTAGE	V0	$V0+V_{in\ max}$

Comparison between conventional boost converter and cuk converter

CHAPTER THREE

Circuit Configuration

The circuit configuration of the proposed converter is presented in figure below.Dp, Dn are two low recovery diodes.D3 is a fast recovery diode.S1,S2 are two main power switches and S_a is the auxiliary switch.

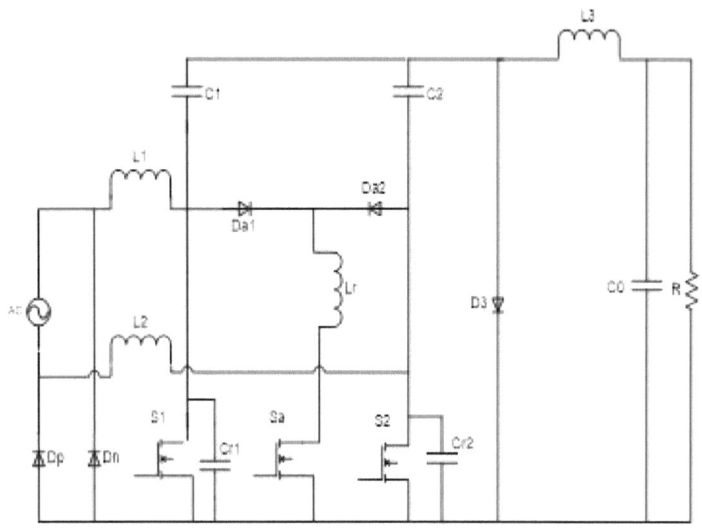

Proposed ZVS bridgeless PWM cuk converter

L1, L2 are the input inductors and L3 is the output inductor. The capacitors C1, C2 are the medium for transferring energy from source to load. The output capacitor C0 is made very large to reduce the output ripple. The auxiliary circuit consists of two auxiliary diodes Da1, Da2 facing each other, one resonant inductor Lr, two resonant capacitors Cr1,Cr2 and one auxiliary switch Sa. The resonant inductance and resonant capacitance are resonant to achieve zero voltage switching (ZVS) of the auxiliary switch. At the same time the resonance between the resonant inductance and output capacitance of the main switches will achieve ZVS of the main switch.One of the main switches and auxiliary switch are all turned on at ZVS which enables the converter to operate with higher switching frequency and reduction in the size of the reactive components.

CHAPTER FOUR

Principle of Operation

Some assumptions of the proposed converter are made in the analysis:

(1) All circuit elements are ideal;

(2) The converter is operating at steady state condition;

(3) The converter operates in continuous conduction mode (CCM);

(4) The output capacitor value is very large to act as an ideal DC voltage source (V0);

(5) Input voltage, input current and output inductor current are constant in a switching cycle.

The operation of the converter is symmetrical in two half line cycles of the input voltage. So the converter operates is explained during the positive half line cycle of the input voltage. There are six operating modes of the proposed converter in a switching period. The current path in all six modes is represented by bold lines. The key waveform is also represented in fig. below. The converter is assumed to operate in a power transferring mode and i_{Lr}=0, V_{Cr}=V_0+$V_{ac}(t_1)$.

Mode 1 (t_1 < t < t_2) : The first mode starts by turning Sa on to provide ZCS condition for the main switch S1.So the L_r current increases linearly with slope of $(V_0+V_{ac}(t_1))/L_r$. This mode lasts until the L_r current reaches i_{in}+i_{L3}.The duration of this mode is obtained by the equation given below.

$$t_2 - t_1 = \frac{(V_0 + V_{ac}(t_1))}{L_r(i_{in} + i_{L3})}$$

Mode 2 (t2 < t < t3): The diode D_3 is turned off under zero current condition, when i_{Lr} reaches i_{in}+i_{L3}.Then resonance between L_r and Cr1 takes place. This mode continues until L_r current becomes zero. The switch S1 can be turned on during this interval. Due to the sinusoidal shape of auxiliary switch S_a, this switch turns on and off under ZCS condition in this mode. To provide soft switching condition i_{Lr} should become zero and below equation need to be satisfied.

$$Z_r \le \frac{(V_0 + V_{in}(t_1))}{i_{in} + i_{L3}}$$

Mode 3 (t3 < t < t4): In this mode,C_r1 is charged by I_{in}+I_{L3} linearly. This mode is finished when the voltage of C_r1reaches zero. So the main switch turns on at ZVS condition. The duration of this mode can be determined from the below equation.

$$t_4 - t_3 = \frac{C_r * V_{cr1}(t_3)}{I_{in} + I_0}$$

Mode 4 (t4 < t < t5):This mode deals with the conducting of the main switch and charging of input inductor which is similar to the on time of the main switch of the conventional hard switching of the cuk converter. This mode lasts until the switch S_1 is turned off.

Mode 5 (t5 < t < t6): This mode starts by turning off the switch S_1.The C_{r1} is charged linearly by the $i_{L3}+i_{in}$ current. Thus the main switch voltage increases linearly to $V_0+V_{in}(t_1)$.At the same time the main switch is turned off under ZVS condition. The following equation describes the duration of this mode.

$$t_6 - t_5 = \frac{C_r(V_0 + V_{in}(t_1))}{I_{in} + I_0}$$

Mode 6 (t6 < t < T_s): In this mode the diode D_3 is turned on under the ZVS condition and the $i_{in}+i_{L3}$ is transferred to the output. This mode continues until the end of the switching cycle T_s.

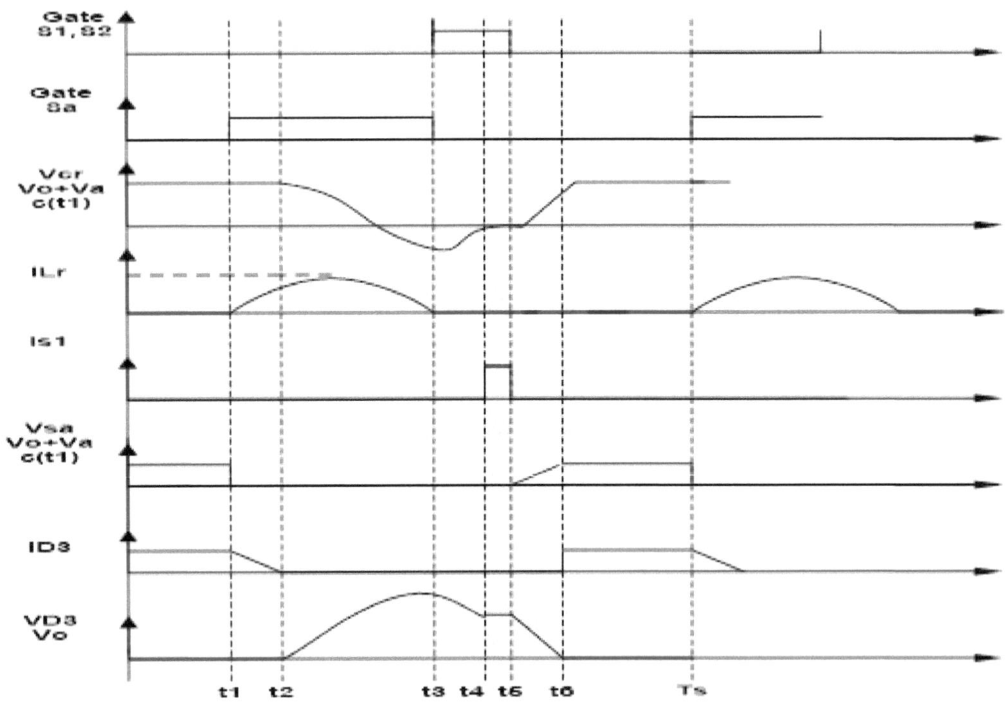

key waveform of proposed converter in ccm

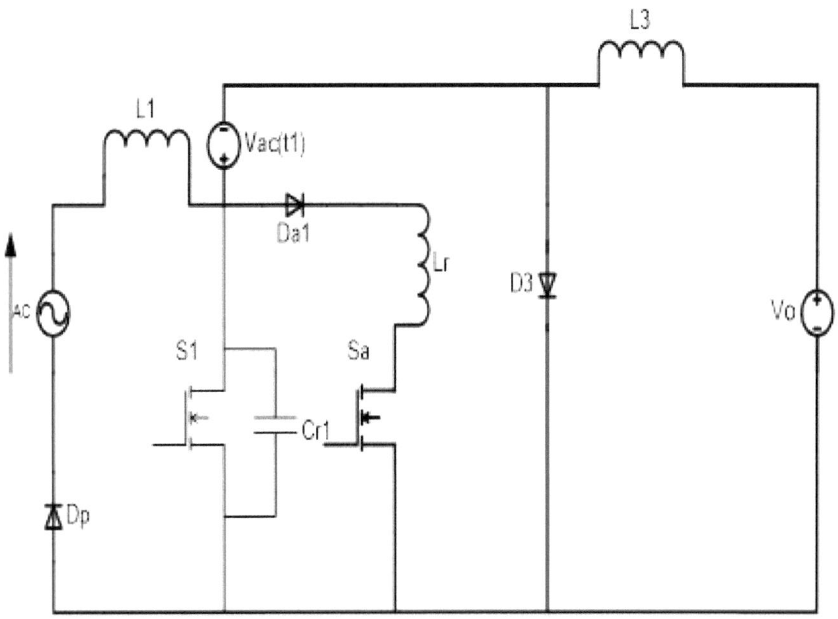

Mode 1 [t1 < t < t2]

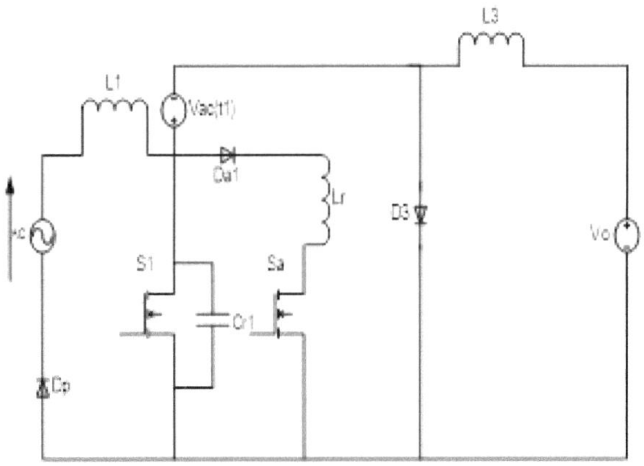

Mode 2 [t2 < t < t3]

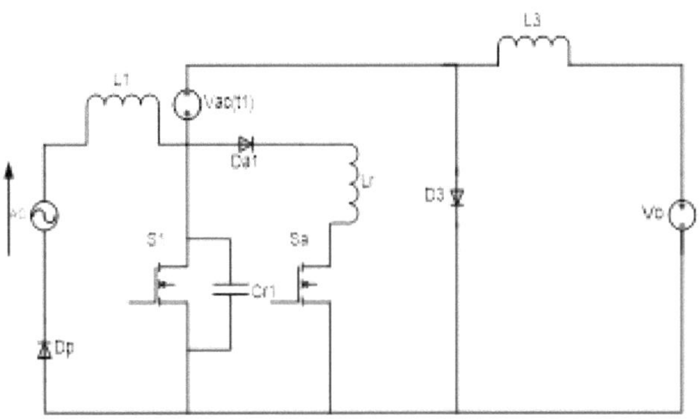

Mode 3 [t3 < t < t4]

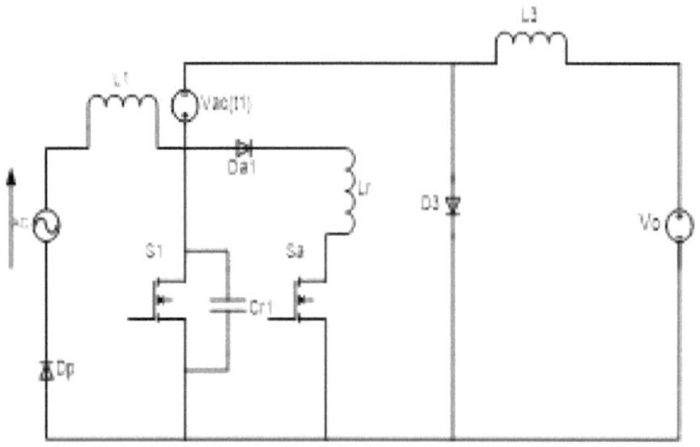

Mode 4 [t4 < t < t5]

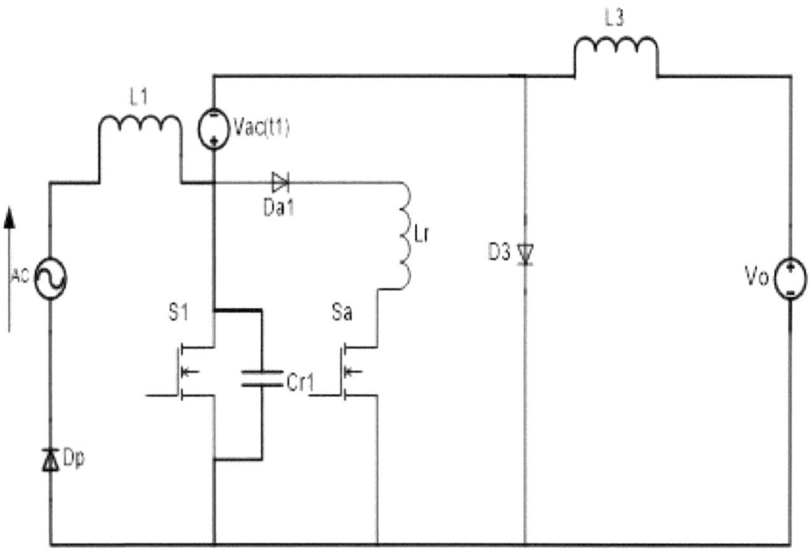

Mode 5 [t5 < t < t6]

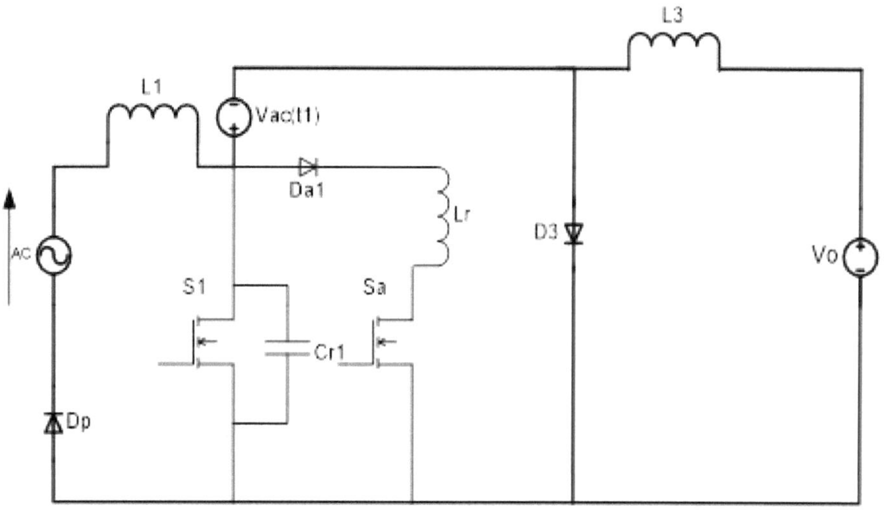

Mode 6 [t6 < t < Ts]

CHAPTER FIVE

Control Scheme

There are two types of the control schemes used in the response improvement of cuk converter .One is input current control and another is output voltage control. Both types of control schemes can be used when the converter is operating in CCM. Depending upon the requirement any of the two can be used. The proposed converter deals with the output voltage regulating scheme as we are interested for the efficiency improvement.

As shown in fig. proportion of output voltage (V'_{out}) is compared with reference voltage and the error signal, thus generated is again compared with a saw tooth waveform to generate the pulse. Finally, this generated pulse is used to drive the gate of the switch. As a result of which the main switches are controlled with respect to the desired output voltage and required high switching frequency. Due to the dual effect of the control signal and soft switching technique, efficiency of the proposed converter has achieved more than 96%.

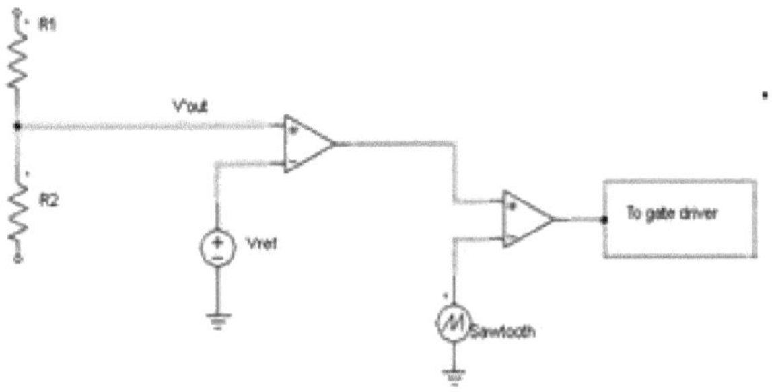

Control circuit for the proposed converter

CHAPTER SIX

Design Consideration

Except at the switching instants the operation of the proposed converter is like conventional cuk converter. The design consideration of the proposed converter is derived from the normal isolated cuk converter. So the design formula for the proposed converter is explained through the formula of isolated cuk converter. The design objective and requirements for the proposed converter are as follows.

- Input voltage ***Vi*** = 85V_{rms}
- Output voltage, **Vo** = 80±5V DC
- Output power, Po = 420W (Max), 380 W (Min)
- Switching frequency, fs = 100kHz
- Transformer turns ration ***N***= 1:1
- Efficiency > 90% for all input voltage and output power conditions
- Peak-peak value of output voltage ripple < 10 V
- Peak-peak value of current ripple on input inductor L1 < 20%, on L2 < 50%

The assumptions required for making the analysis simpler are already discussed in the previous chapter.

<u>Operating Principle of Isolated Ćuk Converter</u>

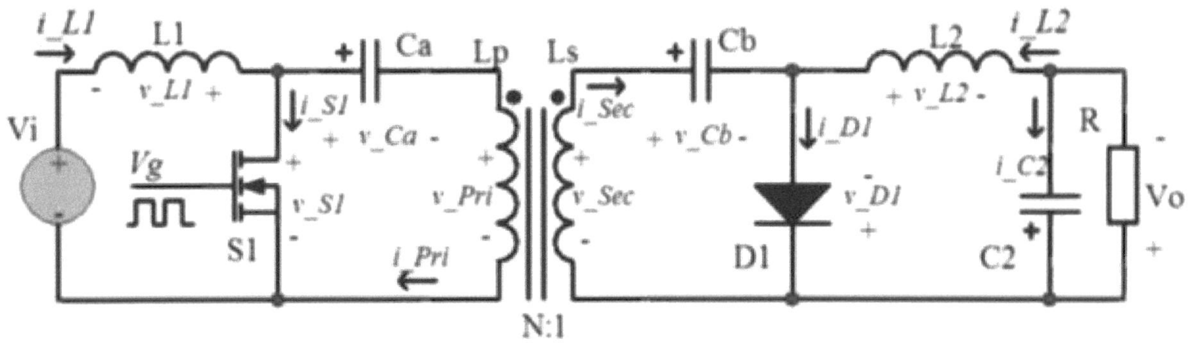

Schematic of Isolated Ćuk Converter

When the switch S1 is on, inductor L1 and the DC source will charge the capacitor Ca. On the secondary side, the current i_Sec will positive and the current of capacitor Cb flows via diode D1. Inductor L2 will release its energy to the load at the same time.

<u>*Using small ripple approximation:*</u>

$V_{L1}=V_{Ca}+V_{pri}-V_i\approx V_{Ca}-V_i$

$V_{L2}=v_0\approx V_0$

$i_{Ca}=i_{L1}\approx I_i$

$i_{Cb}=i_{L1}/N\approx I_i/N$

In order to simplify the analysis, isolated **Ćuk** converter can be equalized to a non-isolated counterpart, which is shown below.

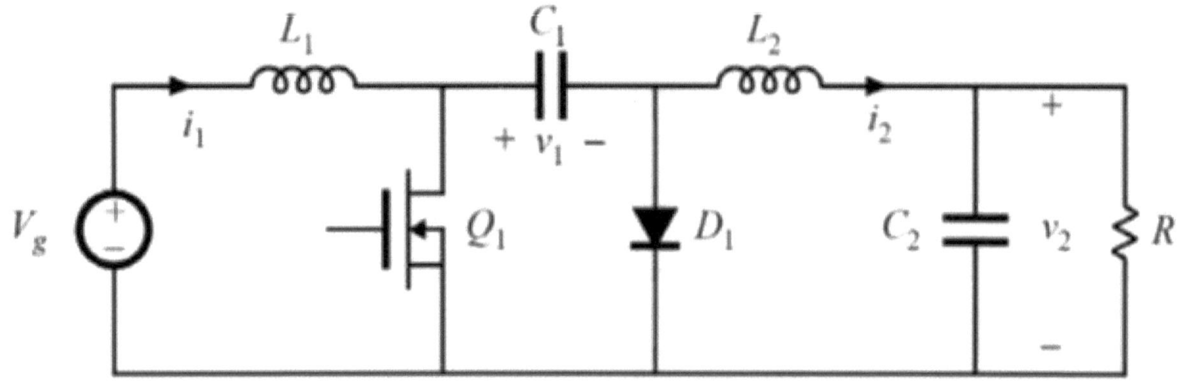

Topology of Non-isolated Ćuk Converter

N=1

$$L2 = \frac{L2'}{N^2}$$

$$C1 = \frac{Ca * N^2 * Cb}{Ca + N^2 * Cb}$$

$$L2 = \frac{L2'}{N^2}$$

C2=N^2*C2'

$$R = V_2^2 / P_0$$

Components Selection:

Detail design value for all the passive (*L1, Ca, Cb, L2, C2*) and active components (S1, D1) to meet the specifications. For inductor: calculate inductance. For capacitor, calculate capacitance and voltage rating. For S1 and D1, calculate current and voltage rating. Get the actual part number.

$$\Delta i_{L1} = \frac{V_g}{2L_1} DT_s$$

$$\Delta i_{L2} = \frac{V_o}{2L_2} D'T_s$$

$$\Delta v_{c1} = \frac{V_o}{2RC} NDT_s$$

$$\Delta v_{c2} = \frac{V_o}{2RC} DT_s$$

$$\Delta v_c = \frac{\Delta i_{L2} T_s}{4C} = \frac{V_o}{8L_2C} D'T_s{}^\wedge 2$$

Using MALAB to calculate the worst condition for the components:

```
clc
Vo=80;
fs=100e3;
Ts=1/fs;
N=1;
L1a=zeros(1,15);
L2a=ones(1,15);
C1a=zeros(1,15);
C2a=zeros(1,15);
Ca=zeros(1,15);
m=0;
delta_vo=10;
for Po=100:100:450 % Considering all the output powers
for Vi=85:12:120 % Considering all the input voltages
m=m+1;
Ro=Vo^2/Po;
k=Vo/Vi;
D=k/(k+N);
delta_iL1=Po/Vi*0.2;
delta_iL2=Po/Vo*0.5;
L1a(m)=Vi*D*Ts/(2*delta_iL1);
L2a(m)=Vo*(1-D)*Ts/(2*delta_iL2);
Vs1=Vi/(1-D);
delta_vC1=Vs1*0.01;
C1a(m)=Vo*N*D*Ts/(2*Ro*delta_vC1);
Vs2=Vo/D;
delta_vC2=Vs2*0.01;
C2a(m)=Vo*D*Ts/(2*Ro*delta_vC2);
Ca(m)=Vo*(1-D)*Ts^2/(8*delta_vo*max(L2a));
end
end
% take twice the max value of L1 and L2 to ensure the ripple requirements
```

```
L1a=2*max(L1a)
L2a=2*max(L2a)
C1a=2*max(C1a)
C2a=2*max(C2a)
Ca=2*max(Ca)
C1=(C1a*N*N*C2a)/(C1a+(N*N*C2a))
L0=L2a/N^2
C0=N^2*C2a
```

<u>So we choose the following parameters for the components:</u>

L1=L2=2.8mH (1)

L3=60μH (2)

C_1=C_2=3.7μF (3)

C_0=1000μF (4)

So the resonant frequency of the auxiliary circuit is selected ten times greater than the switching frequency. The relation between resonant frequency and switching frequency is represented in eq. (5).The values of resonant capacitor and resonant inductor are derived from eq. (5) as Cr1=C_r2=10nF and L_r=5μH.

The value of R1=1.2kΩ.The value of R2 is determined from eq. (6).The value of V_{ref} is normally less than desired output. This value is fixed depending on the output voltage obtained. The phase shift fixed PWM control is provided for auxiliary switch.

$$f_r = \frac{1}{2\pi\sqrt{L_r C_r}} = 0.1 f_{sw} \quad (5)$$

$$R_2 = \frac{R_1 * V_{ref}}{V_0 - V_{ref}} \quad (6)$$

<u>First using MATLAB to get the maximum and minimum value of duty ratio:</u>

```
Vo=80;
N=1;
m=0;
Vi=85:12:120;
D=zeros(1,size(Vi,2));
for Vi=85:12:120
m=m+1;
k=Vo/Vi;
D(m)=k/(k+N);
end
Dmax=max(D)
Dmin=min(D)
```

<u>Matlab Results>></u>

```
Dmax =
0.4848
Dmin =
```

0.4233

POWER EFFICIENCY CALCULATION:

$$\eta = \frac{1}{1+\frac{P_{Loss}}{P_0}}$$

Equation for Efficiency

Using MATLAB to calculate and plot the efficiency

```
Co=500e-12;
rL1=5e-3;
rL2=5e-3;
rDS=5e-3;
rCa=5e-3;
rCb=5e-3;
rCf=5e-3;
rp=5e-3;
rs=5e-3;
L2=1.5e-3;
VrF=2;
f=250e3;
n=1/3;
Po=100:10:600;
P_L1=zeros(1,size(Po));
P_S =zeros(1,size(Po));
P_Ca=zeros(1,size(Po));
P_Tr=zeros(1,size(Po));
P_Cb=zeros(1,size(Po));
P_D=zeros(1,size(Po));
P_L2=zeros(1,size(Po));
P_Cf=zeros(1,size(Po));
PLoss=zeros(1,size(Po));
eff=zeros(1,size(Po));
k=0;
for Po=100:10:600
k=k+1;
Vo=200;
Io=Po/Vo;
Vi=120
Ii=Po/Vi;
R=Vo^2/Po
D=(n*Vo/Vi)/(n*Vo/Vi+1)
P_L1(k)=rL1*D^2*Po/(n^2*R*(1-D)^2);
P_ds=rDS*D*Po/(n^2*R*(1-D)^2);
P_sw=f*Co*n^2*R*Po/D^2;
```

```
P_S(k)=P_ds+P_sw;
P_Ca(k)=rCa*D*Po/(n^2*R*(1-D));
P_Cb(k)=rCb*D*Po/(R*(1-D));
P_Tr(k)=D/(1-D)/R*(rp/n^2+rs)*Po
P_rF=VrF*Io*(1-D)^0.5;
P_vF=VrF/Vo*Po;
P_D(k)=P_rF+P_vF;
P_L2(k)=rL2/R*Po;
P_Cf(k)=rCf*R*(1-D)^2*Po/(12*f^2*L2^2)
PLoss(k)=P_L1(k)+P_S(k)+P_Ca(k)+P_Tr(k)+P_Cb(k)+P_D(k)+P_L2(k)+P_Cf(k)
eff(k)=Po/(Po+PLoss(k))
end
Po=100:10:600;
plot(Po,eff,'g-*')
title('Plot of Efficiency VS. Output Power at Different Input Voltages')
xlabel('Output Power (W)')
ylabel('Efficiency')
```

The figure below gives the plot of efficiency of the converter at different output power.

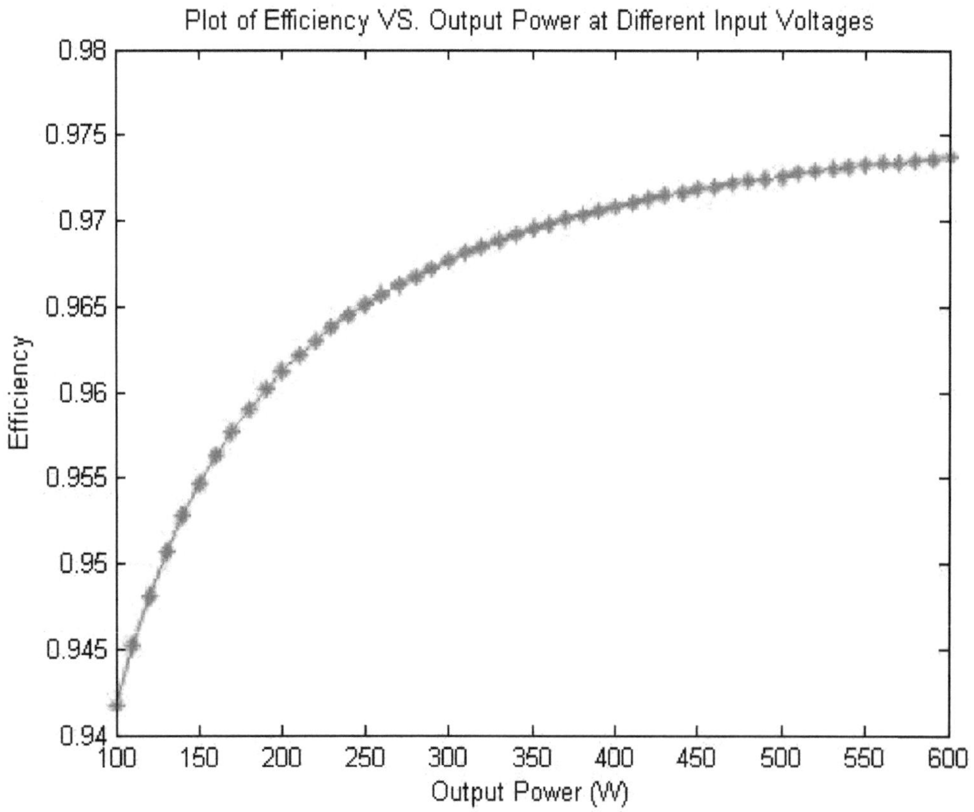

Plot of efficiency VS output power

CHAPTER SEVEN

Simulation Result

The proposed high efficiency bridgeless PWM cuk converter with soft switching technique is simulated by PSIM when V_{AC} =85V_{rms},V_0 =80±5 V_{DC}, f_{SW}=100KHz and 380W output power. By using the design procedure formula the main circuit element values obtained are C_1=C_2=3.7µF, L1=L_2=2.8mH, L3=60µH, C_0=1000µF. The resonant elements, Cr1=C_r2=10nF and L_r=5µH.If we are interested to make the switching transient times observable in the waveforms, then it's better to select resonant frequency 5 times greater than the switching frequency rather following eq. (5) in previous chapter.

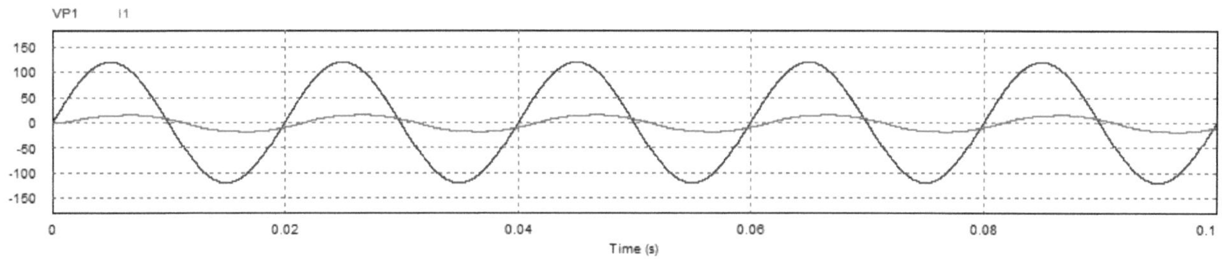

Input voltage & current waveform of the proposed converter

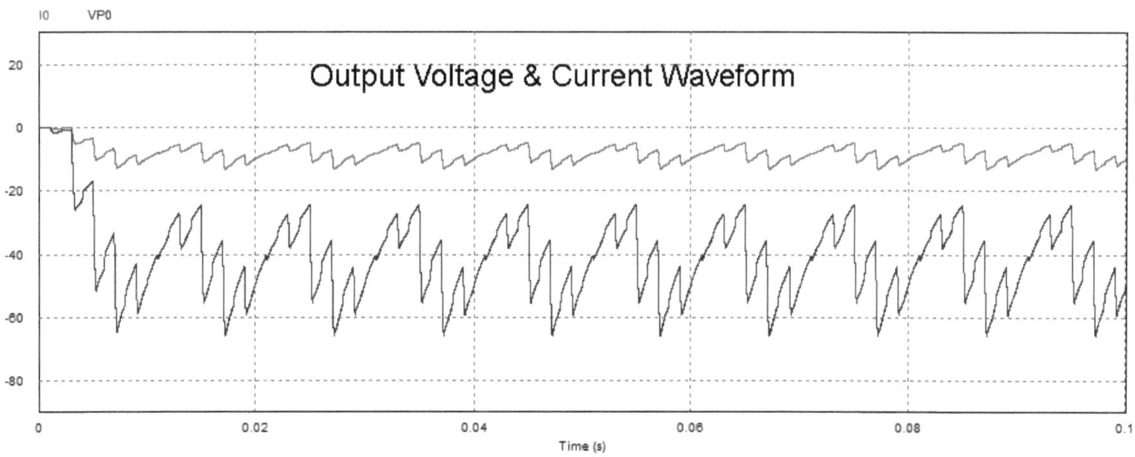

Output voltage & current waveform of the proposed converter

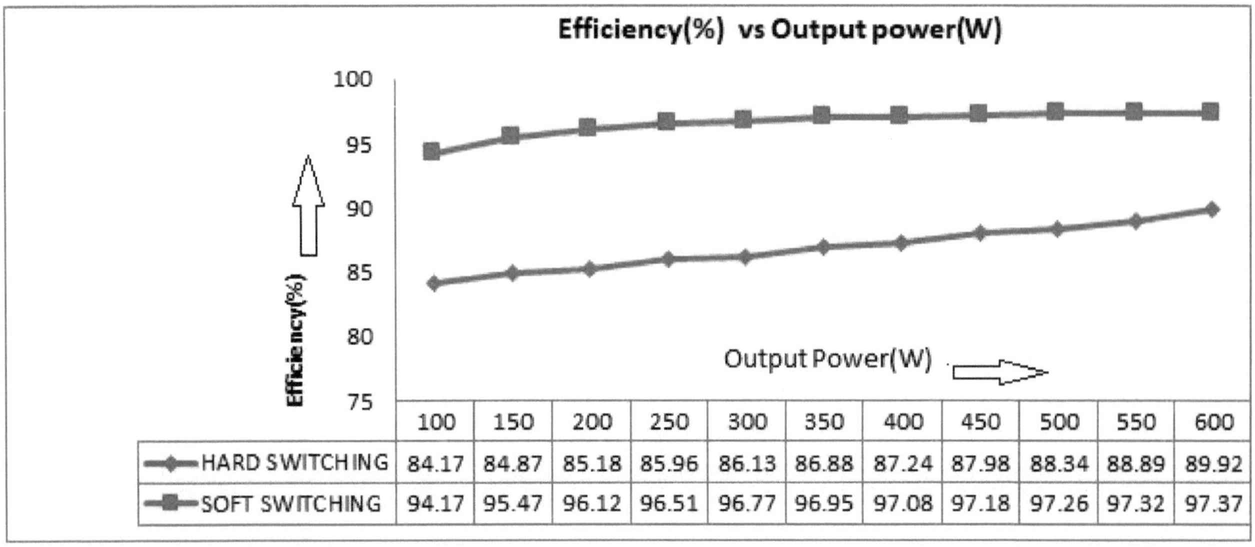

	100	150	200	250	300	350	400	450	500	550	600
HARD SWITCHING	84.17	84.87	85.18	85.96	86.13	86.88	87.24	87.98	88.34	88.89	89.92
SOFT SWITCHING	94.17	95.47	96.12	96.51	96.77	96.95	97.08	97.18	97.26	97.32	97.37

Efficiency Comparison Between Hard Switching & Soft Switching In Proposed Converter

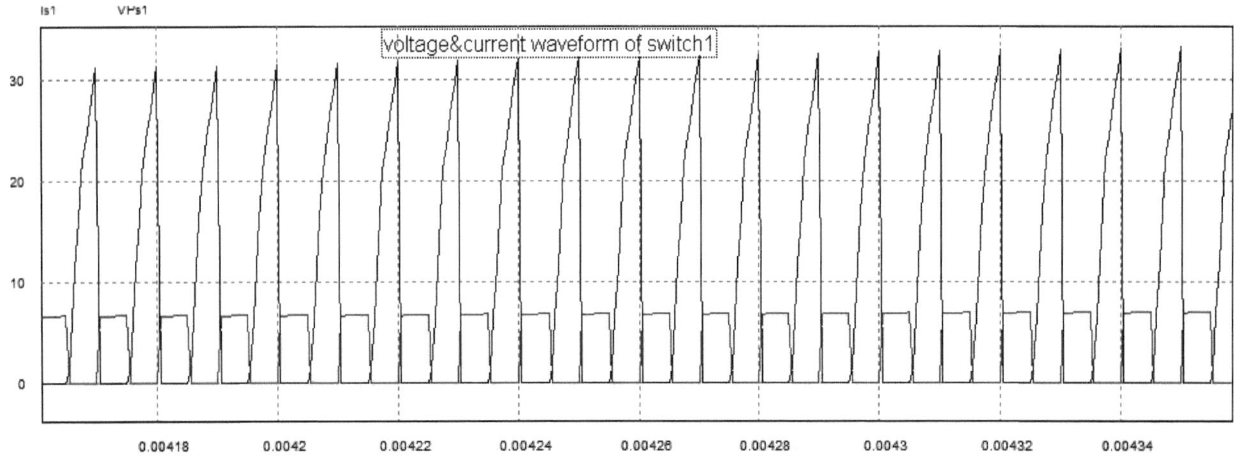

Voltage And Current Waveform Of Switch1 In The Proposed Converter

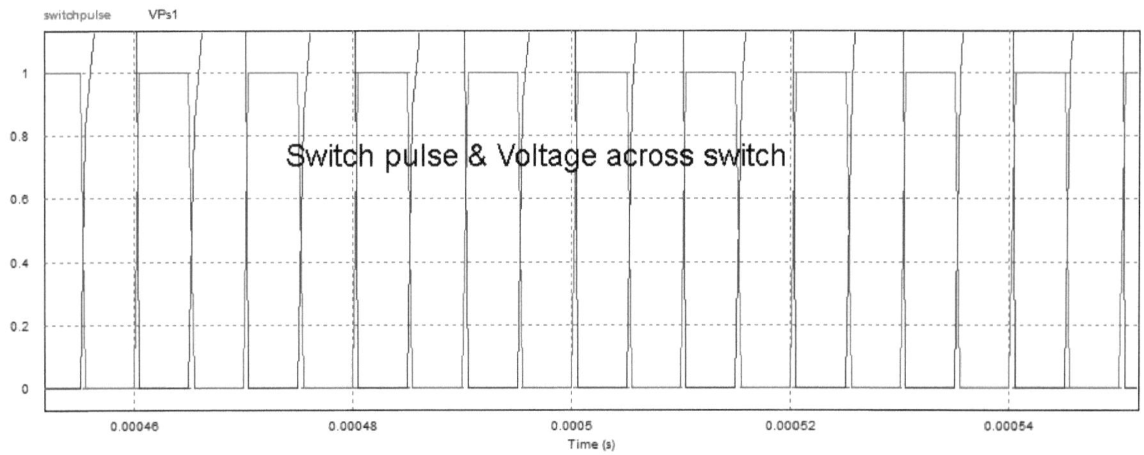

Switching Pulse And Voltage Across Switch Converter

Fig. shows the combined waveform of input current and input voltage. From this waveform it is observed that the input current and input voltages both are almost in phase. It gives almost unity power factor. Fig. gives the combined waveform of the output voltage and current waveform. As the proposed converter is based on soft switching technique, our main attention is on the efficiency improvement. Efficiency comparison between hard switched and soft switched proposed cuk converter obtained from simulation results is presented in figure As discussed in the previous section the use of IGBT as switching device, auxiliary circuit, resonant elements and control circuit enhances the efficiency to a very high value of more than 96%.From the combined waveform of the voltage across and current through the switches . In figure above it is observed that there is no common area between the voltage and current waveform and hence switching loss is also very less. Fig. shows the waveform of switching pulse and voltage across switch. As we know zero voltage switching is the technique in which the switch turns on at zero voltage, the sudden rise and fall of the voltage during turn off and turn on of the main switch says about perfect ZVS of the main switch in the proposed converter.

Conclusion

A new high efficiency bridgeless PWM cuk converter with soft switching technique is introduced in this paper. The main goal of the converter design is efficiency improvement and loss minimization which is verified clearly from the simulation results. Efficiency of more than 96% is obtained. The power factor obtained satisfies the IEC6100-3-2 standard. The input current harmonics is very less. The output voltage regulation helps in getting desired response.

References

1. M.R.Sahid, A.H.M. Yatim and N.D.Muhammad, "A bridgeless Cuk PFC Converter," *IEEE Applied Power Electronics Colloquium (IAPEC),* Publication Year: 2011, Page(s): 81– 85.rans. J. Clerk Maxwell, A Treatise on Electricity and Magnetism, *3rd ed., vol. 2.* Oxford: Clarendon, 1892, pp.68–73.
2. A.A. Fardoun, E.H. Ismail, A.J. Sabzali, M.A.AI-Saffar, "New Efficient Bridgeless Cuk Rectifier for PFC Applications," *IEEE Transaction on Power Electronics,* Page(s): 3292 – 3301.
3. A.J. Sabzali, E.H. Ismail, M.A.AI-Saffar and A.A. Fardoun, "New Bridgeless DCM Sepic and Cuk PFC Rectifier with Low conduction and Switching Losses," *IEEE Trans. on Industry Applications, vol.47,no.2,* pp.873-881,Mar./Apr.2011.
4. M.Mahdavi, H.Farzanehfard, "High efficiency step up/down PFC Rectifier," *International Conference on Applied Electronics,* Publication Year: 2012, Page(s): 179 – 182.
5. B.R.Lin, C.L.Huang, J.F.Wan, "Analysis of a Zero Voltage Switching Cuk Converter," *The 33rd Annual Conference of the IEEE Industrial Electronics Society (IECON),* Publication Year: 2007, Page(s): 1972 –1977.
6. G. Hua, and F. C. Lee, "Soft-switching techniques in PWM converters," *IEEE Trans. Ind. Electron.*, 1995, *vol. 42, no. 6*, pp. 595-603, November 1995.
7. C. A. Canesin, and I. Barbi, "Novel zero-current-switching PWM Converters," *IEEE Trans. Ind. Electron.*, 1997, *vol. 44, no. 3*, pp. 372-381, May 1997.
8. Hancock, J. M, "Bridgeless PFC boost low-line efficiency," *Power Electronics Technology magazine*, February 2008.
9. Woo-Young Choi, Jung-Min Kwon, Kim Eung-Ho, Lee Jong-Jae and Bong-Hwan Kwon, "Bridgeless Boost Rectifier with Low Conduction Losses and Reduced Diode Reverse-Recovery Problems," *Industrial Electronics, IEEE Transactions, Volume: 54*, Publication Year: 2007,Page(s):769 – 780.
10. Mohammad Reza Mohammadi and Hosein Farzanehfard, "A New Bidirectional ZVS-PWM Cuk Converter with Active Clamp," *19thIranian Conference,* Publication Year: 2011, Page(s): 1-6.
11. Masoud Jabbari and Hosein Farzanehfard, "A New Soft Switching Step-Down/Up Converter with Inherent PFC Performance," *Journalof Power Electronics, Vol. 9, No.6*, November 2009.
12. B.-R. Lin1, C.-L. Huang and H.-K. Chiang, "Analysis, design and implementation of an active snubber zero- voltage switching Cuk Converter," *IET Power Electron,* 2008,*Vol.1. No. 1*, pp.50–61.
13. C.-J.Tseng and C.-L.Chen, "Comparisons of zero- voltage-transition Cuk converters," *IEE Proc.-Electr. Power Appl., Vol. 146.No. 4*, July 1999.
14. D. S. L. Simonetti, J. Sebastian, and J. Uceda, "The Discontinuous Conduction Mode Sepic and Cuk Power Factor Preregulators: Analysis and Design," *IEEE Trans. Ind. Electron, vol. 44, no. 5*, Pp.630–637, oct.1997.
15. M. Mahdavi, H. Farzanehfard, "Zero-current-transition bridgeless PFC without extra voltage and current stress,"*IEEE Trans. on Ind. Electron., vol. 56, no. 7*, pp. 2540-2547,Jul. 2009.
16. D.S.L. Simonetti, J. Sebastiin, F. S. dos Reis and J. Uceda, "Design Criteria for Sepic and Cuk Converters as Power Factor Preregulators in Discontinuous Conduction Mode," *International Conference on Power Electronics and*

Motion Control., Publication Year: 1992 , Page(s): 283 - 288 *vol.1*

17. E.Achille, T. Martiré, C. Glaize, and C. Joubert, "Optimized DC-AC boost converters for modular photovoltaic grid-connected generators, "in *Proc. IEEE ISIE'04*, pp. 1005–1010,2004.

18. B.Chitti Babu, R.Vigneshwaran, Sudarshan Karthik, Nayan Ku. Dalei,Rabi Narayan Das, "A Novel Technique for Maximum Power Point Tracking of PV Energy Conversion System', Proc. Of International Conf. on Computer Applications in Electrical Engineering, IIT Roorkee. Pp.276-279, CERA 2010.
19. Bing Lu, Ron Brown, presented at APEC on "Bridgeless PFC Implementation Using One Cycle Control Technique"2005.
20. Huai Wei, *IEEE Member*, and IssaBatarseh, *IEEE Senior Member* "Comparison of Basic Converter Topologies For Power Factor Correction" 1998 IEEE.

****

9 798889 594932

Printed by Libri Plureos GmbH in Hamburg,
Germany